THE ... Y
S...
LunchBox

Sammy Green and Elizabeth Smith

W. Foulsham & Co. Ltd.
London · New York · Toronto · Cape Town · Sydney

Line illustrations by Elaine Hill

W. Foulsham & Company Limited
Yeovil Road, Slough, Berkshire, SL1 4JH

ISBN 0–572–01432–5

Printed in Great Britain at
St Edmundsbury Press,
Bury St Edmunds

CONTENTS

INTRODUCTION

If you are concerned that the nation's children will soon be forming endless queues outside chip vans, sweet shops and fast food outlets, this could be the book for you.

For over a hundred years British schoolchildren have munched their way through soggy semolina and watery cabbage. It may not have been Cordon Bleu but it was regular, hot, filling and cheap at the price. More importantly, we as parents did not have to balance the budget or the food values and someone else did the cooking. But suddenly when most of us are living life in the fast lane and money is tighter than ever, this great British institution, the school dinner, is disappearing.

Do not panic — your child will not end up with rickets and you do not have to be spreading sandwiches at midnight. Our quick and easy recipes are designed to show that, with a little forward planning, you can provide your youngsters with exciting and nutritious food to sustain them through the school year.

We have used only wholefoods in the recipes and kept fat and sugar to a minimum. If you are unfamiliar with the use of wholemeal (whole wheat) flour introduce it gradually, i.e. mix it with white and then move on to 85% as you become used to handling it.

Too much fat in the diet is one of the major health problems of western civilisation and, because we would like to protect our young people, the recipes only include meat occasionally. Fish is an important source of essential oils and therefore we have suggested at least one fish meal per week. Where cheese is used buy the low fat varieties, as Cheddar and other hard cheeses contain high levels of fat. Eggs too have been restricted since a healthy diet should contain no more than 2 or 3 eggs per week.

Each of the school terms is divided into a 4 week cycle and this cycle is repeated throughout the term. To follow the plan we suggest that you cook and freeze the food at some time during the preceding holidays. Or of course you can just use the recipes as you require, to make a change from your routine.

The latest medical research suggests that what our children eat affects their brain function as well as their physical health. Who knows, as you pack their lunch boxes you could be making as major a contribution to their academic achievements as helping with the homework!

Note

Follow one set of measurements only. Do not mix metric, imperial and American measures.

All spoon measurements are level, and are based on a 5 ml teaspoon and a 15 ml tablespoon.

EQUIPMENT

The Lunch Box — What You Need

Kitting out the family for 'lunch boxing' is not expensive, but it is difficult to find wide-necked food flasks suitable for pouring and scooping. Manufacturers have aimed for the junior market with the chunky, 'roughneck' and 'bigmouth', but these cartoon character flasks are not likely to appeal to young sophisticates. However, they are a useful standby for chunky soups and casseroles; shop around for them as the prices vary considerably.

'Thermos' make a 'keep it cool' flask in two sizes. The large 0.5 litre flask, complete with an inner dish for second course, screw top and dish cap flasks, seems to keep food hot satisfactorily. The flask has an all plastic inner and outer casing, but take care because the liner is the traditional glass flask.

Food boxes are worthily cheap but universally dull. Look for deep boxes and well fitting lids. Yoghurt tubs and margarine boxes are very useful for salads and fruit and for freezing small portions of food.

Flasks and boxes may not be colourful but plastic cutlery certainly is. Available in strong red, green, blue and yellow it could add a real party touch.

Cups, beakers and mugs are available in a galaxy of colours, shapes and sizes. Nowhere to be seen in the shops in winter, like flasks and plastic plates and bowls, they emerge with the warmer 'picnic weather', so stock up in June and July with lunch box crocks and cutlery.

Paper napkins or pieces of paper towel are useful for wiping sticky fingers.

A spare plastic bag will be handy for all the scraps, since many schools are short of litter bins and leftovers can cause problems.

Younger members of the family will enjoy having the colourful plastic lunch boxes now available. Older children have not been catered for in the same way. School bags are a fashion item for the young. All we shall advise is that you shop around for a bag that will, with security, contain a food flask and food box. Stationers and design conscious stores are worth exploring when looking for a good bag buy for the smart set 'lunch boxer'.

The Store Cupboard

No one can produce a meal of any sort if the cupboard is bare. During term time it is more important than ever to keep supplies high, unless you happen to have a shop next door which opens before breakfast. The following list will give you a few ideas for useful items.

Baked beans
Wholemeal (whole wheat) or granary bread or rolls
Carob bars
Grated cheese
Cottage cheese
Low-fat, salt-free crisps
Pots of dips and spreads
Hard-boiled (hard-cooked) eggs
Fish paste
Dried fruit
Fresh fruit
Fruit bars
Horseradish sauce
Marmite, Vecon or other concentrated vegetable extracts
Mayonnaise
Mustard
Nuts
Peanut butter
Pickles
Pitta bread
Sardines
Sweetcorn
Tartex
Tuna
Fresh vegetables
Yoghurts

OFF-THE-SHELF MENUS

There are times when the best organised of families are faced with events that disturb the routine. Mum goes down with flu or half the family are sick and the car will not start. At such times the school lunch box has to be thrown together very quickly. This is the time for the 'off-the-shelf menu'. Now that food producers have taken steps to phase out harmful additives and reduce sugar and salt content we can often choose a lunch from cans and jars which, with a little imagination, should keep the family going in its moment of crisis.

SPRING AND SUMMER OFF-THE-SHELF MENUS

MONDAY

* Sandwiches made from thickly-cut wholemeal (whole wheat) bread, a slice of meat left over from Sunday, shredded lettuce, sliced tomato or other salad. If you do not have meat, use chopped hard-boiled (hard-cooked) egg, cucumber, radish and spring onion (scallion) mixed with mayonnaise.
* Low fat yoghurt
* Fruit bar
* Drink

TUESDAY

* Portion of quiche or individual quiche (additive-free varieties are available from supermarkets)
* Wholemeal (whole wheat) roll
* Raw carrot sticks or salad box of sliced red and white cabbage
* Portion of pineapple or melon
* Slice of cake
* Fruit drink

WEDNESDAY

* Pitta bread or bun filled with chopped, grilled beefburger mixed with a teaspoon of tomato ketchup, a sliced tomato and topped with salad. (For older children, try horseradish sauce or mustard instead of ketchup.)
* Fruit yoghurt
* Carob bar
* Drink

THURSDAY

* Can of baked beans mixed with chopped pineapple
* Slice of crusty bread or a roll
* Fruit salad
* Shortbread
* Drink

FRIDAY

* Slice of granary bread
* Pot of dip or spread (available from supermarkets)
* Selection of raw vegetables
* Low-fat, salt-free crisps
* Nuts and raisins
* Fresh fruit
* Drink

MONDAY

* Thin slices of meat spread with cottage cheese and rolled up
* Wholemeal (whole wheat) bread
* Salad of chopped orange, celery and apple
* Tomato
* Nut bar
* A few strawberries
* Drink

TUESDAY

* Thickly-cut granary bread spread with a thin layer of Marmite or Vecon then a thicker layer of peanut butter, topped with thickly-sliced cucumber
* Selection of raw vegetables
* Peach or slice of pineapple
* Scones
* Drink

WEDNESDAY

* Chicken drumstick
* Selection of raw vegetables, such as celery, carrot or cabbage
* Two wholemeal (whole wheat) rolls
* Fresh fruit
* Drink

THURSDAY

* Grilled pizza. Experiment with your own extra toppings such as raw mushrooms, sardines or extra tomatoes.
* Salad of chopped celery, walnut and orange
* Crispbreads and soft cheese
* Fruit salad of plums and grapes
* Fruit drink

FRIDAY

* Fill a roll with mashed, cooked fish cake or fish finger mixed with chopped tomato and a teaspoon of mayonnaise. Top with shredded lettuce and a squeeze of lemon juice.
* Fresh raspberries stirred into a pot of natural yoghurt
* Fruit bar
* Drink

AUTUMN AND WINTER OFF-THE-SHELF MENUS

MONDAY

* Flask of hot soup: vegetable, tomato and goulash are firm favourites
* Chunk of cheese: Dutch cheeses are mild flavoured and chop up quickly and easily
* Granary bread
* Apple or banana
* Fruit drink

TUESDAY

* Flask of hot baked beans, curried or barbecued; mixing two flavours is a good idea.
* Chunks of bread
* Satsumas
* Fruit bar
* Lemonade or a fruit drink

WEDNESDAY

* Hard-boiled (hard-cooked) eggs mixed with chopped tomatoes and salad vegetables. Dress with coleslaw and yoghurt or salad cream. Use to fill sandwiches. Top with lettuce, carrot or raw onion or provide chunks of bread and carrot sticks separately.
* Slice of ginger cake
* Banana
* Flask of hot malted milk drink

THURSDAY

* Flask of hot spaghetti bolognese or macaroni cheese
* Crispbreads or tasty cheese biscuits
* Mince pie
* Apple or orange
* Fruit drink

FRIDAY

* Chunks of wholemeal (whole wheat) bread
* Tub of cottage cheese
* Carrot and celery sticks
* Handful of nuts and raisins with sunflower seeds
* Slice of malt loaf
* Flask of hot cocoa or yeast extract drink

MONDAY

* Egg or vegetable flan or quiche (additive-free var-
  ieties made with vegetable fat are available from
  supermarkets)
* Crisp lettuce leaves and a tomato
* Fruit malt loaf
* Skimmed milk

TUESDAY

* Fish or meat paste generously spread onto granary
  bread buns, topped with a layer of low-fat salt-free
  crisps or a sprinkling of sunflower seeds
* Drinking yoghurt
* Apple
* Mineral water

WEDNESDAY

* Flask of hot spaghetti in tomato sauce
* Slice of crusty bread or a small roll
* Chunk of Cheddar cheese
* Jam or fruit tart
* Banana
* Drink

THURSDAY

* Chopped pineapple (canned in natural juice) mixed with cottage cheese
* Chunks of wholemeal (whole wheat) bread
* Low-fat salt-free crisps
* Slice of ginger cake
* Hot malted milk drink

FRIDAY

* Sausages with a tub of coleslaw and slices of wholemeal bread or sandwiches of sliced sausages with a generous dollop of mild mustard or tomato sauce
* Piece of Kendal Mint Cake or fruit bar
* Pear or apple
* Flask of hot drink

AUTUMN TERM

For most young people September represents a time of change and a new routine. If they are not facing the uncertainties of a new school most certainly they will be facing an unfamiliar teacher. The last thing they will want thrust upon them is strange food. We suggest therefore that if you are a newcomer to wholefoods you introduce a number of these recipes into the family diet before term starts. That way the transition will be gradual and the whole family can enjoy them too.

Autumn is the season when the ubiquitous lettuce, cucumber and tomato salads become more and more expensive. This provides the ideal opportunity to make full use of root vegetables. Turnips, swedes, carrots and parsnips are all delicious grated and sprinkled with a little lemon juice.

To increase the variety of salads, throw in a few raisins, dates or other dried fruits. Seeds such as sunflower, sesame and poppy will all add to the food value as well as providing that extra crunch.

Autumn Term

WEEK 1

Monday	Tomato Quiche * Nutty Murphy (page 115) Gingerbread * (page 90) Grapes Drink
Tuesday	Tim's Tuna Whoppa Salad of Choice (page 110) Carrot Cake * (page 93) Orange Drink
Wednesday	Beany Casserole * Onion Scone * (page 107) Fruit Bar Banana Drink
Thursday	Vegetable Classroom Curry * Granary Bread (page 106) Crunchy Bar Apple Drink
Friday	Student's Tuna and Mushroom Shells Tomato Salad Quick Mix Fruit Cake (page 91) Drink

* suitable for freezing

Tomato Quiche

	Metric	Imperial	American
Makes 8 portions			
Wholemeal (whole wheat) flour	*175 g*	*6 oz*	*1½ cups*
Baking powder	*2 tsp*	*2 tsp*	*2 tsp*
Vegetable margarine	*100 g*	*4 oz*	*½ cup*
Water	*3 tbsp*	*3 tbsp*	*3 tbsp*
Vegetable oil	*1 tbsp*	*1 tbsp*	*1 tbsp*
Onion, chopped	*1*	*1*	*1*
Curd cheese or quark (small curd cottage cheese)	*225 g*	*8 oz*	*1 cup*
Eggs, beaten	*3*	*3*	*3*
Tomatoes, chopped	*4*	*4*	*4*
Skimmed milk	*4 tbsp*	*4 tbsp*	*4 tbsp*
Ground black pepper			
Dried mustard	*½ tsp*	*½ tsp*	*½ tsp*

1. Sift the flour and baking powder into a bowl and rub in the margarine until the mixture resembles fine breadcrumbs.
2. Make a well in the centre and add the water. Mix until the dough forms a ball, cover and refrigerate for 30 minutes.
3. Meanwhile, heat the oil in a saucepan and fry the onion until soft. Leave to cool.
4. Roll out the pastry and use to line an 18 cm/7 inch flan ring. To bake blind, line base with greaseproof (waxed) paper and weigh down with dried beans. Bake in the oven at 190°C/375°F/Gas Mark 5 for 10 minutes.
5. Remove the beans and bake for a further 10 minutes.
6. Place the remaining ingredients in a bowl and blend.
7. Line the base of the flan with the cooked onion. Pour in the tomato and cheese mixture and bake for a further 20 minutes.

Tim's Tuna Whoppa

	Metric	Imperial	American
Makes 4			
Wholemeal (whole wheat) batons (a section of wholemeal French bread may be used)	*4 large*	*4 large*	*4 large*
Vegetable margarine	*50 g*	*2 oz*	*¼ cup*
Onion, finely chopped	*1 small*	*1 small*	*1 small*
Canned pilchards, chopped	*75 g*	*3 oz*	*⅓ cup*
Natural yoghurt	*2 tbsp*	*2 tbsp*	*2 tbsp*
Canned tuna fish, chopped	*75 g*	*3 oz*	*⅓ cup*
Carrot, grated	*1 small*	*1 small*	*1 small*

1. Cut the rolls into 3 sections lengthways. Do not cut straight through, you should be left with 2 cavities to fill. Spread with the margarine.
2. Mix the onion, pilchards and 1 tablespoon of the yoghurt. Fill one of the sections of each of the rolls with the mixture.
3. Mix the tuna, carrot and the remaining yoghurt and use to fill the second section.

Note: The older the child the more exciting you can make the fillings. They might enjoy the addition of a little mustard or mayonnaise.

Beany Casserole

	Metric	Imperial	American
Makes 4 portions			
Onion, sliced	*1 large*	*1 large*	*1 large*
Carrot, sliced	*1 large*	*1 large*	*1 large*
Parsnip, cubed	*1*	*1*	*1*
Water	*450 ml*	*¾ pint*	*2 cups*
Vegetable margarine	*25 g*	*1 oz*	*2 tbsp*
Wholemeal (whole wheat) flour	*25 g*	*1 oz*	*¼ cup*
Milk	*about 300 ml*	*about ½ pint*	*about 1¼ cups*
Cooked haricot beans (navy beans), canned may be used, but rinse before use	*275 g*	*8 oz*	*1⅓ cups*
Canned tomatoes	*400 g*	*14 oz*	*16 oz*
Tomato purée	*2 tbsp*	*2 tbsp*	*2 tbsp*
Vecon or concentrated vegetable extract	*1 tsp*	*1 tsp*	*1 tsp*
Dried mustard	*½ tsp*	*½ tsp*	*½ tsp*

1. Cook the onion, carrot and parsnip in the water until soft. Drain and reserve the stock.
2. Melt the margarine in a saucepan, stir in the flour and cook gently for 2 minutes.
3. Slowly add the stock, made up to 600 ml/1 pint/2 cups with the milk and stir until thickened.
4. Stir in the remaining ingredients and the cooked vegetables. Simmer gently for 10 minutes.

Note: Transport in a wide-necked flask.

Vegetable Classroom Curry

	Metric	Imperial	American
Makes 4 portions			
Vegetable oil	*2 tbsp*	*2 tbsp*	*2 tbsp*
Onion	*1 medium*	*1 medium*	*1 medium*
Potato, scrubbed and cubed	*1 large*	*1 large*	*1 large*
Carrots, sliced	*2 medium*	*2 medium*	*2 medium*
Turnip, cubed	*1 small*	*1 small*	*1 small*
Cauliflower, broken into florets	*1 small*	*1 small*	*1 small*
Green pepper, deseeded and sliced	*1*	*1*	*1*
Cooked chick peas	*100 g*	*4 oz*	*⅔ cup*
Ground coriander	*1 tsp*	*1 tsp*	*1 tsp*
Ground cumin	*1 tsp*	*1 tsp*	*1 tsp*
Turmeric	*1 tsp*	*1 tsp*	*1 tsp*
Cayenne pepper	*½ tsp*	*½ tsp*	*½ tsp*
Chilli powder (optional)	*½ tsp*	*½ tsp*	*½ tsp*
Water	*600 ml*	*1 pint*	*2½ cups*
Canned tomatoes	*425 g*	*15 oz*	*16 oz*
Bulgar wheat	*100 g*	*4 oz*	*⅔ cup*
Sultanas (golden raisins)	*50 g*	*2 oz*	*⅓ cup*

1. Heat the oil in a saucepan and fry the onion until soft.
2. Add all the vegetables and chick peas (canned peas should be rinsed first) and stir over a moderate heat until just beginning to brown.
3. Add all the spices and cook for a further 2 minutes. Carefully add the water and tomatoes, stirring continuously.
4. Stir in the bulgar wheat and sultanas and cook gently until vegetables are cooked, about 20 minutes.

Note: Any vegetables in season can be used and the hotness adjusted to suit the child's taste. Transport in a wide-necked flask.

Student's Tuna and Mushroom Shells

	Metric	Imperial	American
Makes 4 portions			
Wholemeal (whole wheat) pasta shells	*175 g*	*6 oz*	*6 oz*
Vegetable oil	*2 tbsp*	*2 tbsp*	*2 tbsp*
Onion, chopped	*1*	*1*	*1*
Green pepper, deseeded and chopped	*1 small*	*1 small*	*1 small*
Button mushrooms, sliced	*100 g*	*4 oz*	*1 cup*
Milk or natural yoghurt	*150 ml*	*¼ pint*	*⅔ cup*
Canned tuna fish, drained and flaked	*200 g*	*7 oz*	*1 cup*
Ground black pepper			

1. Cook the pasta shells in a large pan of boiling water with 1 tablespoon of the oil until just soft, about 10 minutes. Drain.
2. Heat the remaining oil in a saucepan and fry the onion until soft, about 5 minutes. Add the pepper and mushrooms and cook for 2 minutes.
3. Stir in the pasta with the milk and tuna. Season and heat through.

Note: Transport in a wide-necked flask.

Tomato Salad

	Metric	Imperial	American
Tomatoes, sliced	2	2	2
Chopped parsley			
Lemon juice			

1. Place the tomatoes in a plastic container and sprinkle with a little parsley and lemon juice to taste.

Note: A little dressing may be used instead of lemon juice. Choose firm tomatoes.

Autumn Term

WEEK 2

Monday

Pocket Pasty *
Carrot and Orange Salad (page 115)
Gingerbread * (page 90)
Nutty Yoghurt (page 101)
Drink

Tuesday

Spinach and Cottage Cheese Quiche *
Raw Mushrooms or Salad of Choice (page 110)
Fruity Compote * (page 92)
Nut Bar
Drink

Wednesday

Spicy Red Beans *
Granary Bread (page 106)
Carrot Cake * (page 93)
Melon
Drink

Thursday

Prefect's Pizza *
Rooty Vegetables (page 111)
Quick Mix Fruit Cake * (page 91)
Apple
Drink

Friday

Triple Decker Sardine and Salad Sandwich
Mark's Munch (page 112)
Nut Bar
Banana
Drink

* suitable for freezing

Pocket Pasties

	Metric	Imperial	American
Makes 6 pasties			
Lean meat, diced	*450 g*	*1 lb*	*2 cups*
Raw potato, diced	*175 g*	*6 oz*	*1 cup*
Celery, chopped	*2 tbsp*	*2 tbsp*	*2 tbsp*
Onion, chopped	*1 small*	*1 small*	*1 small*
Ground black pepper			
Mixed herbs (optional)	*1 tsp*	*1 tsp*	*1 tsp*
Wholemeal (whole wheat) pastry	*450 g*	*1 lb*	*1 lb*
Milk to glaze			

1. Combine the meat, potato, celery and onion. Season with pepper and herbs, if using.
2. Roll out the pastry to form 6 rounds. Place a portion of the meat mixture on each.
3. Dampen the edges of the pastry and draw together to form a pasty shape. Brush with milk.
4. Bake in the oven at 220°C/425°F/Gas Mark 7 for 15 minutes. Reduce the heat to 160°C/325°F/Gas Mark 3 for a further 45 minutes.
5. Cool and freeze if necessary.

Note: For curried pasties, add 1 teaspoon curry powder to the meat mixture.

Spinach and Cottage Cheese Flan

	Metric	Imperial	American
Makes 6 generous portions			
PASTRY			
Raw cane sugar	*1 tsp*	*1 tsp*	*1 tsp*
Wholemeal (whole wheat) flour	*225 g*	*8 oz*	*8 oz*
Vegetable fat (shortening)	*50 g*	*2 oz*	*2 oz*
Vegetable margarine (solid margarine)	*50 g*	*2 oz*	*2 oz*
Cold water	*2 tbsp*	*2 tbsp*	*2 tbsp*
FILLING			
Frozen creamed spinach, thawed	*225 g*	*8 oz*	*1 cup*
Cottage cheese	*225 g*	*8 oz*	*1 cup*
Eggs, beaten	*2*	*2*	*2*
Coriander, freshly ground	*½ tsp*	*½ tsp*	*½ tsp*
Sprinkling of cayenne pepper			
Chopped parsley			

1. Mix the sugar into the flour.
2. Add the fats, cut with a knife then rub into the flour. Mix in the water then roll the pastry into a ball. Put aside to rest for 30 minutes.
3. Roll out on a floured board. Handle lightly as the mixture will crumble more easily than a standard white pastry.
4. Line a 23 cm/9 inch flan dish or tin (pan) with the pastry. To bake blind, line base with greaseproof (waxed) paper and weigh down with dried beans. Bake in the oven at 190°C/375°F/Gas Mark 5 for 10 minutes.

5. Meanwhile, thaw the spinach over a very gentle heat or allow to thaw at room temperature.
6. Stir into the thawed spinach the cottage cheese, eggs and the spices.
7. Spoon into the flan case and bake in the oven at 160°C/325°F/Gas Mark 3 for 30–40 minutes.
8. Sprinkle with parsley. Serve hot or cold.

Spicy Red Beans

	Metric	Imperial	American
Makes 4 portions			
Sunflower oil	*3 tbsp*	*3 tbsp*	*3 tbsp*
Onions, chopped	*2*	*2*	*2*
Green pepper, deseeded and chopped	*1*	*1*	*1*
Canned red kidney beans	*425 g*	*15 oz*	*16 oz*
Canned tomatoes	*397 g*	*14 oz*	*16 oz*
Slices fresh pineapple, cubed	*2*	*2*	*2*
Tomato purée	*4 tbsp*	*4 tbsp*	*¼ cup*
Paprika	*2 tsp*	*2 tsp*	*2 tsp*
Chilli (chili) powder	*¼ tsp*	*¼ tsp*	*¼ tsp*
Ground black pepper			

1. Heat the oil in a saucepan and sauté the onion until soft.
2. Add the green pepper and cook for a further 3 minutes.
3. Stir in the remaining ingredients adding black pepper to taste. Cook gently for 15 minutes.
4. When cool freeze in 4 polythene plastic bags ready to defrost and reheat as needed.

Note: Transport in a wide-necked flask.

Prefect's Pizza

	Metric	Imperial	American
Makes 4 × 15 cm/6 inch pieces			
Easy bake dried yeast	*1 pkt*	*1 pkt*	*1 pkt*
Brown sugar	*1 tsp*	*1 tsp*	*1 tsp*
Wholemeal (whole wheat) flour	*450 g*	*1 lb*	*4 cups*
Egg	*1*	*1*	*1*
Sunflower oil	*150 ml*	*¼ pint*	*⅔ cup*
Warm water	*about 400 ml*	*about ⅔ pint*	*about 1¾ cups*
TOPPING			
Vegetable oil	*2 tbsp*	*2 tbsp*	*2 tbsp*
Onion, chopped	*1*	*1*	*1*
Green pepper, deseeded and chopped	*½ small*	*½ small*	*½ small*
Mushrooms, sliced	*100 g*	*4 oz*	*1 cup*
Canned tomatoes	*397 g*	*14 oz*	*16 oz*
Tomato purée	*2 tbsp*	*2 tbsp*	*2 tbsp*
Basil	*½ tsp*	*½ tsp*	*½ tsp*
Oregano	*½ tsp*	*½ tsp*	*½ tsp*
Ground black pepper			
Cheese, grated	*75 g*	*3 oz*	*¾ cup*

1. In a large bowl stir the yeast and sugar into the flour.
2. Beat the egg with the oil and sufficient warm water to make up to 400 ml/⅔ pint/1¾ cups. Pour in the liquid and stir to form a dough. Gather the dough together with your hands and knead on a floured board for 10 minutes. This is a part which is easily delegated.
3. Cut the dough into 4 equal portions and roll out to form round pizzas, about 5 mm/¼ inch thick. Cover with a polythene (plastic) bag and leave in a warm place to rise, about 30 minutes.
4. Meanwhile make the topping. Heat the oil in a sauce-

pan and sauté the onion until soft, about 5 minutes. Add the green pepper and cook for a further 3 minutes.

5. Add the mushrooms, tomatoes, purée and herbs and simmer gently until the sauce becomes a thick pulp. Add black pepper to taste.
6. Spoon the mixture over the pizza bases and sprinkle with the cheese. Bake in the oven at 220°C/425°F/Gas Mark 7 for 12–15 minutes.

Note: These pizzas freeze well.

Triple Decker Sardine and Salad Sandwich

	Metric	Imperial	American
Makes 2 portions			
Can sardines (smoked mackerel or tuna are just as tasty)	*120 g*	*4 ¼ oz*	*4 oz*
Lemon juice			
Ground black pepper			
Lettuce, shredded			
Mustard and cress (optional)			
Apple, sliced (Granny Smith are good)	*1*	*1*	*1*
Granary (whole wheat) bread	*4 slices*	*4 slices*	*4 slices*

1. Mix the fish with lemon juice and black pepper to taste.
2. Place layers of lettuce, mustard and cress and apple on the slices of bread, topped up with the fish mixture, to form a triple decker salad.

To vary, mix fish with quark spread (small curd cottage cheese) or mayonnaise.

Autumn Term

WEEK 3

Monday
Vegetable Hash *
Wholemeal (Whole wheat) Bread
Brie (or other low fat cheese)
Quick Mix Fruit Cake * (page 91)
Grapes
Drink

Tuesday
Peanut Burger in a Bun *
Green Salad (page 114)
Fruity Yoghurt (page 100)
Gingerbread * (page 90)
Drink

Wednesday
Pitta Parcels *
Chinese Salad (page 112)
Nut Bar
Orange
Drink

Thursday
Playtime Pasties *
Red Salad (page 114)
Fruity Compote * (page 92)
Walnut and Banana Cake (page 92)
Drink

Friday
Mermaid's Delight Pâté *
Wholemeal (Whole wheat) Toast
Cauliflower Salad (page 116)
Carrot Cake * (page 93)
Orange
Drink

* suitable for freezing

Vegetable Hash

	Metric	Imperial	American
Makes 4 portions			
Yellow split peas	175 g	6 oz	¾ cup
Sunflower or corn oil	2 tbsp	2 tbsp	2 tbsp
Onions, chopped	2 large	2 large	2 large
Carrots, cut into chunks	2	2	2
Stalks celery, chopped	2	2	2
Potatoes, washed and chopped	2	2	2
Swede (rutabaga), chopped	¼	¼	¼
Vegetable stock (bouillon) cube	1	1	1
Water	300–450 ml	½–¾ pint	1¼–2 cups
Ground black pepper			
Bay leaf (optional)			

1. Pick over the split peas and soak in hot water for 30 minutes. Drain.
2. Heat the oil slightly in a large pan or wok. Add the onion and allow to soften but not brown. Cook for 10 minutes, stirring from time to time.
3. Add the remaining vegetables. Cook for another 10 minutes, stirring.
4. Dissolve the stock cube in the water and add to the vegetables with the split peas. Add pepper to taste and bay leaf. Bring to boil then turn down the heat and simmer for an hour.
5. Lift out the vegetables with a slotted spoon. Purée the split peas. Return vegetables to purée mixture. Serve like a hearty soup.

Note: Transport in a wide-necked flask.

Peanut Burger in a Bun

	Metric	Imperial	American
Makes 6 burgers			
Vegetable oil	1 tbsp	1 tbsp	1 tbsp
Onion, chopped	1 small	1 small	1 small
Wholemeal (whole wheat) breadcrumbs	100 g	4 oz	1 cup
Crunchy peanut butter	400 g	4 oz	½ cup
Tomato purée	1 tbsp	1 tbsp	1 tbsp
Soy sauce	1 tsp	1 tsp	1 tsp
Mixed herbs	1 tsp	1 tsp	1 tsp
Ground black pepper			
Sesame seeds	2 tsp	2 tsp	2 tsp
Wholemeal (whole wheat) rolls or baps	6	6	6

1. Heat the oil in a saucepan and sauté the onion until soft, about 5 minutes.
2. Stir the onion and oil into the breadcrumbs, peanut butter, tomato purée, soy sauce and herbs. Mix well and add pepper to taste.
3. Form into 6 burgers and coat with the sesame seeds. Grill until the sesame seeds are brown and crisp.
4. When the burgers are cold cut open the rolls and fill.

Note: You can freeze the rolls filled or freeze separately and assemble on the day.

Pitta Parcels

Pitta bread can make a welcome change from a sandwich. The wholemeal (whole wheat) variety is now available in most supermarkets and health food shops. Buy a few packets at a time and store in the freezer.

To fill the pitta simply slit the side with a sharp knife and pop in the filling of your choice. The suggestions below will each fill 4 pittas. Small appetites may only require half a bread.

Baked Bean and Tomato Filling

	Metric	Imperial	American
Canned baked beans	450 g	1 lb	16 oz
Horseradish sauce	2 tsp	2 tsp	2 tsp
Tomatoes, chopped	2	2	2
Cucumber, chopped	1 tbsp	1 tbsp	1 tbsp

1. Mash the beans, stir in the other ingredients and pack the pittas.

Spicy Peanut Butter Filling

	Metric	Imperial	American
Crunchy peanut butter (if possible use the unsalted variety)	5 tbsp	5 tbsp	5 tbsp
Natural yoghurt	2 tbsp	2 tbsp	2 tbsp
Small onion, chopped	1	1	1
Chilli (chili) powder	pinch	pinch	pinch
Soy sauce	1 tsp	1 tsp	1 tsp

1. Mix all the ingredients together and pack the pittas.
2. Add fresh salad ingredients on the morning you pack the lunch.

Cottage Cheese and Mint Filling

	Metric	Imperial	American
Cottage cheese	225 g	8 oz	1 cup
Fresh garden mint, chopped	2 tbsp	2 tbsp	2 tbsp
Tomato, chopped	1	1	1
Cucumber, chopped	2 tbsp	2 tbsp	2 tbsp

1. Mix all the ingredients together and pack the pittas.

Playtime Pasties

	Metric	Imperial	American
Makes 4 pasties			
Wholemeal (whole wheat) flour	*225 g*	*8 oz*	*2 cups*
Baking powder	*2 tsp*	*2 tsp*	*2 tsp*
Vegetable margarine	*100 g*	*4 oz*	*½ cup*
Cold water	*3 tbsp*	*3 tbsp*	*3 tbsp*
Onion, chopped	*1*	*1*	*1*
Carrot, chopped	*1*	*1*	*1*
Potato, cubed	*1 large*	*1 large*	*1 large*
Turnip or swede (rutabaga), cubed	*50 g*	*2 oz*	*⅓ cup*
Vecon or concentrated vegetable extract	*1 tsp*	*1 tsp*	*1 tsp*
Leftover cooked meat, minced, or cooked lentils	*50 g*	*2 oz*	*¼ cup*
Ground black pepper			

1. Place the flour and baking powder in a bowl and rub in the margarine until the mixture resembles bread-crumbs. Mix in the water until you have a firm dough. Cover and leave to rest in the refrigerator for 30 minutes.
2. Mix all the vegetables and Vecon with the meat or lentils. Add pepper to taste.
3. Divide the pastry into 4 portions and roll out into circles on a floured board. Dampen the edges of each circle and place ¼ of the vegetable mixture on each.
4. Fold over and seal each pasty and bake in the oven at 200°C/400°F/Gas Mark 6 for 15 minutes. Reduce the oven to 160°C/325°F/Gas Mark 3 for a further 15 minutes.

Mermaid's Delight Pâté

	Metric	Imperial	American
Makes 2 portions			
Canned pink salmon	*100 g*	*3 ½ oz*	*3 ½ oz*
Cottage cheese	*75 g*	*3 oz*	*scant ⅓ cup*
Lemon juice			
Ground black pepper			

1. Mix together the salmon and cottage cheese. Add lemon juice and pepper to taste.

   This pâté is excellent with vegetable sticks or spread on granary or wholemeal (whole wheat) bread. For a 'hold in the hand' meal try pitta bread filled with this pâté, adding grated carrot and other salad vegetables.

Autumn Term

WEEK 4

Monday	Pasta with Vegetables Wholemeal (Whole wheat) Roll Fruity Yoghurt (page 100) Crunchy Bar Drink
Tuesday	Cheese Scones (page 108) Winter Salad (page 115) Quick Mix Fruit Cake * (page 91) Apple or Banana Drink
Wednesday	Cream of Split Pea Soup * Onion Scone * (page 107) Gingerbread * (page 90) Melon Drink
Thursday	Daniel's Chilli con Carne * Wholemeal (Whole wheat) Bread Fruity Compote * (page 92) Nut Bar Drink
Friday	Mackerel Pâté * Raw Vegetable Sticks Wholemeal (Whole wheat) Bread Carrot Cake (page 93) Grapes Drink

* suitable for freezing

Pasta with Vegetables

	Metric	Imperial	American
Makes 4 portions			
Wholemeal (whole wheat) pasta spirals	*275 g*	*10 oz*	*2½ cups*
Vegetable oil	*1 tsp*	*1 tsp*	*1 tsp*
Vegetable oil for frying	*2 tbsp*	*2 tbsp*	*2 tbsp*
Onion, chopped	*1*	*1*	*1*
Celery stalks, sliced	*2*	*2*	*2*
Red pepper, deseeded and chopped	*½*	*½*	*½*
Courgettes (zucchini), sliced	*3 medium*	*3 medium*	*3 medium*
Canned tomatoes	*397 g*	*14 oz*	*16 oz*
Sunflower seeds	*50 g*	*2 oz*	*½ cup*
Ground black pepper			

1. Cook the pasta in a large pan of boiling water with the 1 teaspoon oil until tender, about 10 minutes.
2. Heat the remaining oil in a saucepan and fry the onion until softened. Add the remaining vegetables and the tomatoes and cook until a pulp forms.
3. Add the seeds and black pepper to taste. Heat through.
4. Drain the pasta and stir into the sauce.

Note: Any nuts or small pieces of leftover lean chicken or meat can be added to this dish. Transport in a wide-necked flask.

Cream of Split Pea Soup

	Metric	Imperial	American
Makes 6–8 portions			
Yellow split peas	*100 g*	*4 oz*	*1½ cups*
Sunflower oil	*1 tbsp*	*1 tbsp*	*1 tbsp*
Onion, finely chopped	*1 medium*	*1 medium*	*1 medium*
Clove garlic, crushed (optional)	*1*	*1*	*1*
Potato, diced	*1 large*	*1 large*	*1 large*
Celery stalks, diced	*2*	*2*	*2*
Ground coriander	*¼ tsp*	*¼ tsp*	*¼ tsp*
Ground black pepper	*½ tsp*	*½ tsp*	*½ tsp*
Bay leaf	*1*	*1*	*1*
Stock or water	*750–900 ml*	*1¼–1½ pints*	*3–3¾ cups*

1. Soak the split peas in hot water for 30 minutes. Drain.
2. Heat the oil in a large pan or wok and gently fry the onion and garlic for 3–4 minutes.
3. Add the potato, celery, split peas, coriander and black pepper. Cook for another 5 minutes, stirring occasionally.
4. Add the bay leaf and most of the stock or water. Bring to boil, cover and simmer for 40 minutes.
5. Liquidize, adding more stock if too thick.

Note: Transport in a wide-necked flask.

Daniel's Chilli Con Carne

	Metric	Imperial	American
Makes 4 portions			
Vegetable oil	*1 tbsp*	*1 tbsp*	*1 tbsp*
Onion, chopped	*1*	*1*	*1*
Green pepper, deseeded and chopped	*½*	*½*	*½*
Lean minced (ground) beef (try using TVP as a replacement, or 75 g/3 oz meat plus 75 g/3 oz TVP)	*175 g*	*6 oz*	*1¾ cups*
Oregano	*1 tsp*	*1 tsp*	*1 tsp*
Chilli (chili) powder, depending on taste	*½–2 tsp*	*½–2 tsp*	*½–2 tsp*
Canned red kidney beans, drained	*397 g*	*14 oz*	*16 oz*
Canned tomatoes	*397 g*	*14 oz*	*16 oz*
Tomato purée	*2 tbsp*	*2 tbsp*	*2 tbsp*

1. Heat the oil in a saucepan and fry the onion until soft. Add the green pepper and cook for a further 2 minutes.
2. Stir in the meat and cook for 2 more minutes.
3. Add the oregano, chilli powder, beans, tomatoes and tomato purée. Cook until the meat is tender.

Note: TVP stands for textured vegetable protein (meat extender) and is available from health food shops. Transport in a wide-necked flask.

Mackerel Pâté

	Metric	Imperial	American
Makes 4 portions			
Smoked mackerel fillets	*2 large*	*2 large*	*2 large*
Cream cheese	*100 g*	*4 oz*	*½ cup*
Lemon juice	*1 tsp*	*1 tsp*	*1 tsp*
Natural yoghurt	*150 ml*	*5 fl oz*	*⅔ cup*
Ground black pepper			

1. Mash the mackerel into the cream cheese.
2. Stir in the lemon juice and yoghurt. Add pepper to taste.
3. Divide into 4 pots.

Note: This freezes well and is delicious served with raw vegetable sticks.

THE EASTER TERM

The first half of the Easter term is probably the coldest part of the year. It is the time when chill winds, lashing rain and sub zero temperatures render the mere idea of an egg sandwich ludicrous. With careful planning during the pre-term week your freezer can supply hot and nutritious meals to combat winter weather.

Hearty soups and casseroles are the basis of this term's menus. Once you have settled into the routine of preparing the lunches in advance you should find it easy to invent your own recipes suitable for flasks.

Keep a plentiful supply of cooked beans in your freezer ready for instant use. I periodically cook large quantities and pack them into 450g/1lb and 225g/½lb bags so that I can always throw a bean casserole together at short notice. Canned beans are perfectly all right as long as you remember to rinse the brine off first, but of course they are a lot more expensive than cooking your own.

Energy requirements are greatest during the winter both to fulfil the games curriculum and to keep warm, so do not forget to provide plentiful supplies of wholemeal (whole wheat) bread and do convince your weight-conscious sons and daughters that bread and potatoes are not necessarily fattening. It is what accompanies them that needs watching.

Easter Term

WEEK 1

Monday	Chicken Risotto * Cheese Scone * (page 108) Fruity Bread Pudding (page 96) Satsuma Drink
Tuesday	Leek and Butter Bean Soup * Granary Bread (page 106) Apricot Slice * (page 99) Apple Drink
Wednesday	Cashew Slice * Wholemeal (Whole wheat) Roll Red Salad (page 114) Apple Crunch (page 97) Grapes Drink
Thursday	Potato Pea Hot Pot Wholemeal (Whole wheat) Bread Citrus Yoghurt (page 101) Carob Brownie * (page 98) Drink
Friday	Chicken and Mushroom Pies Potato, Radish and Nut Salad (page 116) Fruit Bar Drink

* suitable for freezing

Chicken Risotto

	Metric	Imperial	American
Makes 4 portions			
Sunflower oil	*3 tbsp*	*3 tbsp*	*3 tbsp*
Onions, chopped	*2*	*2*	*2*
Celery stalks, sliced	*2*	*2*	*2*
Cooked brown rice	*450 g*	*1 lb*	*3 cups*
Cooked peas	*100 g*	*4 oz*	*¾ cup*
Cooked lean chicken, diced	*175–225 g*	*6–8 oz*	*scant 1 cup*
Sultanas (golden raisins)	*50 g*	*2 oz*	*⅓ cup*
Tomatoes, chopped	*100 g*	*4 oz*	*½ cup*
Ground black pepper			

1. Heat the oil in a saucepan and sauté the onion until transparent. Add the celery and stir-fry for 5 more minutes.
2. Add the remaining ingredients one at a time, stirring well.
3. When the risotto is thoroughly heated through remove from the heat.

Note: Any leftover vegetables or meat can be added to this. If the child enjoys spicier food 1 teaspoon each of ground cumin and ground coriander can be added. Transport in a wide-necked flask.

Leek and Butter Bean Soup

	Metric	Imperial	American
Makes 6–8 portions			
Butter beans (dried lima beans), soaked overnight	*225 g*	*8 oz*	*¾ cup*
Leeks, thoroughly washed, split lengthways and chopped	*450 g*	*1 lb*	*1 lb*
Onion, chopped	*1*	*1*	*1*
Bay leaves	*2*	*2*	*2*
Ground black pepper	*½ tsp*	*½ tsp*	*½ tsp*
Vegetable stock or water	*900 ml*	*1½ pints*	*3¾ cups*

1. Drain the butter beans and place them in a large pan with about 900 ml/1½ pints/3¾ cups of water. Bring to rapid boil and keep on the boil for 10 minutes. Reduce heat, keeping the beans at a steady simmer for 30 minutes. Remove from heat and drain.
2. Mix the leeks, onion, bay leaves and black pepper with the butter beans, adding the vegetable stock or water. Simmer for 1 hour.

Note: This is a hearty soup served as it is. For a thicker soup, liquidize to required taste. Transport in a wide-necked flask.

Cashew Slice

	Metric	Imperial	American
Makes 10 slices			
Vegetable fat (shortening)	*25 g*	*1 oz*	*2 tbsp*
Onions, chopped	*2 medium*	*2 medium*	*2 medium*
Cashews, ground	*225 g*	*8 oz*	*2 cups*
Wholemeal (whole wheat) breadcrumbs	*100 g*	*4 oz*	*1 cup*
Eggs, beaten	*2*	*2*	*2*
Chopped parsley	*1 tbsp*	*1 tbsp*	*1 tbsp*
Skimmed milk	*150 ml*	*¼ pint*	*⅔ cup*
Ground black pepper			

1. Melt the fat in a saucepan and sauté the onion until brown.
2. Mix the remaining ingredients together and combine with the onion. The mixture should be fairly stiff.
3. Line a 1 kg/2 lb loaf tin (9 × 5 inch loaf pan) with non-stick parchment and pour in the nut and onion mixture.
4. Bake in the oven at 200°C/400°F/Gas Mark 6 for 40 minutes.
5. When cold, slice into portions. Use one for the packed lunch and freeze the remainder.

Potato Pea Hot Pot

	Metric	Imperial	American
Makes 4 portions			
Vegetable oil	*2 tbsp*	*2 tbsp*	*2 tbsp*
Onions, sliced	*2 medium*	*2 medium*	*2 medium*
New potatoes, washed and diced	*225 g*	*8 oz*	*1⅓ cups*
Peas, fresh or frozen	*100 g*	*4 oz*	*¾ cup*
Carrots, sliced	*2*	*2*	*2*
Red lentils	*100 g*	*4 oz*	*½ cup*
Canned tomatoes	*397 g*	*14 oz*	*16 oz*
Vegetable stock (bouillon) cube	*1*	*1*	*1*
Rolled oats	*25 g*	*1 oz*	*⅓ cup*

1. Heat the oil in a saucepan and sauté the onion until soft.
2. Add the potatoes, peas and carrots and stir fry for 2 or 3 minutes more.
3. Stir in the lentils and tomatoes. Crumble in the stock cube and simmer until the vegetables are tender, about 25 minutes. If the mixture becomes too dry add a little water or vegetable stock.
4. Stir in the rolled oats which will thicken the hot pot and cook for a further 10 minutes.
5. When cool pack into bags for the freezer.

Note: Transport in a wide-necked flask.

Chicken and Mushroom Pies

	Metric	Imperial	American
Makes 4 pies			
Vegetable oil	*1 tbsp*	*1 tbsp*	*1 tbsp*
Onion, chopped	*1*	*1*	*1*
Mushrooms, sliced	*50 g*	*2 oz*	*½ cup*
Wholemeal (whole wheat) shortcrust pastry	*225 g*	*8 oz*	*½ lb*
Cooked chicken, chopped	*225 g*	*8 oz*	*1 cup*
Tomato, chopped	*1*	*1*	*1*
Milk to glaze			

1. Heat the oil in a saucepan and sauté the onion until soft, about 5 minutes. Add the mushrooms, cook for a further 2–3 minutes then leave to cool.
2. Roll out two thirds of the pastry and use to line 4 small pie dishes.
3. Add the chicken and tomato to the onion and mushrooms and mix well. Use to fill the pies.
4. Roll out the remaining pastry and cut out 4 lids. Dampen the edges and place over the pies.
5. Bake in the oven at 220°C/425°F/Gas Mark 7 for 15–20 minutes until cooked and golden.

Note: To vary the vegetables, substitute chopped celery or carrot.

Easter Term

Monday	Buck's Pasty * Sweet and Crunchy Cauliflower (page 111) Apricot Slice * (page 99) Nutty Yoghurt (page 101) Drink
Tuesday	Schoolroom Scotch Egg * (page 53) Green Salad (page 114) Wholemeal (Whole wheat) Roll Carob Brownie * (page 98) Satsuma Drink
Wednesday	Cheese and Tomato Bites (page 54) Raw Vegetable Sticks Winter Fruit Salad (page 102) Satchel Snack (page 102) Drink
Thursday	Magic Bean Soup * (page 51) Cheese Scone * (page 108) Fruity Bread Pudding * (page 96) Banana Drink
Friday	Fishy Pizza * (page 52) Rooty Vegetables (page 111) Apple Crunch * (page 97) Orange Drink

*suitable for freezing

Buck's Pasties

	Metric	Imperial	American
Makes 4 substantial pasties			
PASTRY			
Vegetable fat (shortening)	*50 g*	*2 oz*	*¼ cup*
Vegetable margarine	*50 g*	*2 oz*	*¼ cup*
Granary or wholemeal (whole wheat) flour	*225 g*	*8 oz*	*2 cups*
Cold water	*2 tbsp*	*2 tbsp*	*2 tbsp*

1. Rub the fats into the flour.
2. Add the water, stir into the flour with a knife then mix with the fingers. Roll the pastry into a ball.
3. Place on floured board and roll out. Handling the pastry carefully, cut into 4 and form large rounds.
4. Put some filling onto each piece of pastry, damp the edges and form into pasty shapes. Seal the edges.
5. Bake in the oven at 220°C/425°F/Gas Mark 7 for 10 minutes, then reduce the oven temperature to 180°C/350°F/Gas Mark 4 for 15 minutes.

PASTY FILLING

	Metric	Imperial	American
Split peas	*100 g*	*4 oz*	*½ cup*
Potatoes, scrubbed and diced	*225 g*	*8 oz*	*1½ cups*
Swede (rutabaga), diced	*100 g*	*4 oz*	*⅔ cup*
Carrots, chopped	*100 g*	*4 oz*	*⅔ cup*
Onion, sliced	*100 g*	*4 oz*	*1 cup*
Yeast extract, dissolved in a little hot water	*1 generous tsp*	*1 generous tsp*	*1 generous tsp*

	Metric	Imperial	American
Ground black pepper mixed with ground coriander	½ tsp	½ tsp	½ tsp
Water	450 ml	¾ pint	2 cups

1. Pick over the split peas and rinse. Cover with boiling water and soak for 30 minutes. Drain.
2. Place all the vegetables, soaked split peas, yeast extract, seasoning and water in a casserole.
3. Cook in the oven at 150°C/300°F/Gas Mark 2 for 1½ hours. The vegetables should have absorbed most of the liquid. Let mixture cool before filling pasties.

This vegetable mixture is also useful as a base for a thick and hearty soup. Simply add more water.

For extra flavour, sprinkle some chopped fresh chives over the filling before baking the pasties.

Magic Bean Soup

	Metric	Imperial	American
Makes 6 portions			
Can baked beans	450 g	16 oz	16 oz
Can tomatoes	397 g	14 oz	16 oz
Onion, chopped	1 large	1 large	1 large
Carrot, chopped	1	1	1
Celery stalks	2	2	2
Water	1.2 litres	2 pints	5 cups
Worcestershire sauce	1 tsp	1 tsp	1 tsp
Ground black pepper			

1. Place all the ingredients in a large saucepan and simmer gently until the vegetables are tender, about 20–30 minutes.
2. Purée the soup in a blender or liquidizer and serve with chunks of wholemeal (whole wheat) bread.

Note: Transport in a wide-necked flask.

Fishy Pizza

	Metric	Imperial	American
Makes 4 × 15 cm/6 inch pizzas			
Easy bake dried yeast	*1 pkt*	*1 pkt*	*1 pkt*
Brown sugar	*1 tsp*	*1 tsp*	*1 tsp*
Wholemeal (whole wheat) flour	*450 g*	*1 lb*	*4 cups*
Egg	*1*	*1*	*1*
Sunflower oil	*150 ml*	*¼ pint*	*⅔ cup*
Warm water	*300–400 ml*	*½–⅔ pint*	*1¼–1¾ cups*

TOPPING

	Metric	Imperial	American
Sunflower oil	*2 tbsp*	*2 tbsp*	*2 tbsp*
Onion, chopped	*1 medium*	*1 medium*	*1 medium*
Green pepper, deseeded and chopped	*½*	*½*	*½*
Tomato purée	*2 tbsp*	*2 tbsp*	*2 tbsp*
Canned tomatoes	*397g*	*14 oz*	*16 oz*
Oregano	*½ tsp*	*½ tsp*	*½ tsp*
Basil	*½ tsp*	*½ tsp*	*½ tsp*
Ground black pepper			
Pilchards, chopped	*225 g*	*8 oz*	*1 cup*
Cheese, grated	*75 g*	*3 oz*	*¾ cup*

1. In a large bowl stir the yeast and sugar into the flour.
2. Mix the egg with the oil and sufficient water to make up to 300–400 ml/½–⅔ pint/1¼–1¾ cups. Pour the liquid into the flour mixture and stir to form a dough. Gather the dough using your hands and knead on a floured board for 10 minutes.
3. Cut the dough into 4 equal portions and roll out to form round pizzas, about 5 mm/¼ inch thick. Place on a greased baking tray, cover with a polythene

(plastic) bag and leave in a warm place to rise, about 30 minutes.
4. Meanwhile, heat the oil in a saucepan and sauté the onion until soft, about 5 minutes. Add the green pepper and cook for a further 3 minutes.
5. Add the remaining ingredients except the pilchards and cheese and simmer gently until the sauce becomes a thick pulp.
6. Spoon the mixture over the pizza bases. Dot the surface with pilchards and cover with grated cheese. Bake in the oven at 220°C/425°F/Gas Mark 7 for 12–15 minutes.

Schoolroom Scotch Eggs

	Metric	Imperial	American
Makes 4			
Water	*300–450 ml*	*½–¾ pint*	*1¼–2 cups*
Vegetarian sausage mix	*225 g*	*8 oz*	*½ lb*
Chopped parsley	*1 tsp*	*1 tsp*	*1 tsp*
Onion, chopped	*2 tsp*	*2 tsp*	*2 tsp*
Worcestershire sauce	*dash*	*dash*	*dash*
Eggs, hard-boiled (hard-cooked)	*4*	*4*	*4*
Vegetable or sunflower oil for deep frying			

1. Mix the water into the sausage mix and leave to stand for 5 minutes. This should give a stiff consistency.
2. Add the parsley, onion and Worcestershire sauce and stir well.
3. Mould the mixture around the eggs, taking care to seal the edges.
4. Deep fry the eggs in oil until golden brown. Drain on kitchen paper.

Cheese and Tomato Bites

	Metric	Imperial	American
Makes 6–8 pieces			
Cheddar cheese, grated	*225 g*	*8 oz*	*2 cups*
Tomatoes, chopped	*2 large*	*2 large*	*2 large*
Raisins	*25 g*	*1 oz*	*3 tbsp*
Lemon juice			
Wholemeal (whole wheat) short-crust pastry	*225 g*	*8 oz*	*½ lb*
Milk to glaze			

1. Mix together the cheese, tomatoes and raisins. Sprinkle with a little lemon juice.
2. Roll out the pastry and cut into 7.5–10 cm/3–4 inch circles.
3. Dampen the edges and place a spoonful of cheese mixture on each. Draw the edges together to seal and brush with a little milk.
4. Bake in the oven at 200°C/400°F/Gas Mark 6 for 10–15 minutes, until golden brown.

Easter Term

WEEK 3

Monday   Vegetable Warmer Soup *
                  Cheese Scone * (page 108)
                  Apricot Slice * (page 99)
                  Grapes
                  Drink

Tuesday   Matron's Savoury Loaf *
                  Wholemeal (Whole wheat) Roll
                  Cucumber and Apple Salad (page
                      115)
                  Satchel Snack (page 102)
                  Pear
                  Drink

Wednesday   Triple Decker Chicken and Cheese
                      Sandwich
                  Fruit Salad
                  Carob Brownie * (page 98)
                  Drink

Thursday   Baked Bean Wedge *
                  Sweet and Crunchy Cauliflower
                      (page 111)
                  Fruity Yoghurt (page 100)
                  Bar
                  Drink

Friday   Master's Macaroni *
                  Wholemeal (Whole wheat) Roll
                  Apple Crunch (page 97)
                  Satsuma
                  Drink

* suitable for freezing

Vegetable Warmer Soup

	Metric	Imperial	American
Makes 6–8 portions			
Corn oil	*2 tbsp*	*2 tbsp*	*2 tbsp*
or butter	*25 g*	*1 oz*	*2 tbsp*
Onion, chopped	*1 large*	*1 large*	*1 large*
Leeks, split, chopped and thoroughly washed	*2*	*2*	*2*
Turnip, sliced	*1 small*	*1 small*	*1 small*
Celery stalks, chopped	*3*	*3*	*3*
Potatoes, quartered	*2 large*	*2 large*	*2 large*
Water	*600 ml*	*1 pint*	*2½ cups*
Salt and pepper			
Milk	*300 ml*	*½ pint*	*1¼ cups*

1. Heat the oil or butter in a saucepan and cook the onion gently until soft, about 5 minutes. Do not brown.
2. Stir in the leeks, turnip and celery. Cover and cook slowly over a low heat, stirring occasionally. Leave over a low heat for 15 minutes or until vegetables are soft.
3. Add the potatoes with the water and salt and pepper to taste. Simmer until the vegetables are tender, about 20 minutes.
4. Add the milk, simmer for a few more minutes until thoroughly heated through.

Note: Transport in a wide-necked flask.

Matron's Savoury Loaf

	Metric	Imperial	American
Makes 8 portions			
Vegetable margarine	25 g	1 oz	2 tbsp
Onions, chopped	2 medium	2 medium	2 medium
Mushrooms, sliced	100 g	4 oz	1 cup
Wholemeal (whole wheat) flour	275 g	10 oz	1½ cups
Milk	150 ml	¼ pint	⅔ cup
Lean minced (ground) beef	450 g	1 lb	2 cups
Wholemeal (whole wheat) breadcrumbs	175 g	6 oz	1½ cups
Tomato purée	3 tbsp	3 tbsp	3 tbsp
Mixed herbs	1 tsp	1 tsp	1 tsp
Chopped parsley	1 tbsp	1 tbsp	1 tbsp
Eggs, beaten	2	2	2
Worcestershire sauce	1 tsp	1 tsp	1 tsp
Parmesan cheese, grated	25 g	1 oz	¼ cup

1. Melt the margarine in a saucepan and sauté the onions until soft. Add the mushrooms and flour and cook for 2 minutes, stirring constantly.
2. Slowly add the milk and bring to the boil. Remove from the heat.
3. Add all the remaining ingredients and pack into a 500 g/1 lb loaf tin (7 x 3 inch loaf pan).
4. Bake in the oven at 200°C/400°F/Gas Mark 6 for 1 hour.
5. When cool slice and pack for the freezer.

Triple Decker Chicken and Cheese Sandwich

	Metric	Imperial	American
Makes 1 sandwich			
Granary (whole wheat) bread	*3 slices*	*3 slices*	*3 slices*
Vegetable margarine for spreading			
Mayonnaise or yoghurt	*1 tbsp*	*1 tbsp*	*1 tbsp*
Cooked chicken, chopped	*50 g*	*2 oz*	*¼ cup*
Pineapple, diced	*25 g*	*1 oz*	*2 tbsp*
Edam or Cheddar cheese, grated	*25 g*	*1 oz*	*¼ cup*
Raisins	*1–2 tbsp*	*1–2 tbsp*	*1–2 tbsp*
A little mustard (optional)			
Shredded lettuce			

1. Spread 2 slices of bread with margarine.
2. Mix the mayonnaise or yoghurt with the chicken and pineapple. Spread this on the third piece of bread.
3. Mix the cheese and raisins and the mustard if used and spread on one of the first 2 slices.
4. Assemble the sandwich alternating with the shredded lettuce.

Baked Bean Wedge

	Metric	Imperial	American
Makes 4 portions			
Canned baked beans (look for the sugar-free varieties)	*446 g*	*16 oz*	*16 oz*
Wholemeal (whole wheat) breadcrumbs	*150 g*	*5 oz*	*1¼ cups*
Cheese, grated	*175 g*	*6 oz*	*1½ cups*
Onion, chopped	*1*	*1*	*1*
Mixed herbs	*2 tsp*	*2 tsp*	*2 tsp*
Egg, beaten	*1*	*1*	*1*

1. Mash the beans and breadcrumbs together.
2. Mix in the other ingredients to form a stiff dough. If it is too thick it can be thinned down with a little milk.
3. Pack into the base of an 18 cm/7 inch greased cake tin (pan). Bake in the oven at 160°C/325°F/Gas Mark 3 for about 1 hour.
4. When cold cut into 4 wedges.

Master's Macaroni

	Metric	Imperial	American
Makes 4 portions			
Vegetable fat (shortening)	25 g	1 oz	2 tbsp
Onion, chopped	1	1	1
Carrot, chopped	1	1	1
Celery stalk, sliced	1	1	1
Green pepper, deseeded and diced	½	½	½
Basil	1 tsp	1 tsp	1 tsp
Oregano	1 tsp	1 tsp	1 tsp
Tomato purée	2 tbsp	2 tbsp	2 tbsp
Canned tomatoes	400 g	14 oz	16 oz
Ground black pepper			
Wholemeal (whole wheat) macaroni	225 g	8 oz	2 cups
Vegetable oil	1 tsp	1 tsp	1 tsp
Cooked green lentils	100 g	4 oz	½ cup

1. Melt the fat in a saucepan and sauté the onion until soft, about 5 minutes.
2. Add the carrot, celery and green pepper and stir fry for a further 5 minutes.
3. Stir in the herbs, tomato purée, tomatoes and black pepper to taste. Cook for approximately 20 minutes until the vegetables are tender.
4. Meanwhile cook the macaroni in a large pan of boiling water until tender, about 10 minutes. Add the 1 teaspoon of oil to prevent the pasta from sticking. Drain and return to the pan.
5. Stir the sauce and cooked lentils into the macaroni. Warm through gently.

Note: Transport in a wide-necked flask.

Easter Term

Monday   Peanut Pie *
Winter Salad (page 115)
Fruity Bread Pudding * (page 96)
Banana
Drink

Tuesday   Tomato, Orange and Celery
Soup *
Cheese Scone * (page 108)
Fruit Salad
Carob Brownie * (page 98)
Drink

Wednesday   Curried Nut Loaf *
Mark's Munch (page 112)
Apricot Slice * (page 99)
Apple
Drink

Thursday   Pasta and Vegetable Salad
Wholemeal (Whole wheat) Bread
Apple Crunch * (page 97)
Orange
Drink

Friday   German Sausage Sandwich
Granary Bread (page 106)
Fruity Yoghurt (page 100)
Bar
Drink

* suitable for freezing

Peanut Pies

	Metric	Imperial	American
Makes 4			
Vegetable margarine	*100 g*	*4 oz*	*½ cup*
Wholemeal (whole wheat) flour	*225 g*	*8 oz*	*2 cups*
Baking powder	*2 tsp*	*2 tsp*	*2 tsp*
Cold water	*3 tbsp*	*3 tbsp*	*3 tbsp*
FILLING			
Vegetable oil	*1 tbsp*	*1 tbsp*	*1 tbsp*
Onion, chopped	*1*	*1*	*1*
Wholemeal (whole wheat) breadcrumbs	*100 g*	*4 oz*	*1 cup*
Crunchy peanut butter	*100 g*	*4 oz*	*½ cup*
Carrot, grated	*1*	*1*	*1*
Tomato purée	*1 tbsp*	*1 tbsp*	*1 tbsp*
Soy sauce	*1 tsp*	*1 tsp*	*1 tsp*
Mixed herbs	*1 tsp*	*1 tsp*	*1 tsp*
Cracked wheat	*25 g*	*1 oz*	*scant ¼ cup*
Cheese, grated	*75 g*	*3 oz*	*¾ cup*
A little milk to glaze			

1. Rub the margarine into the flour until the mixture resembles breadcrumbs.
2. Stir in the baking powder. Make a well in the centre of the flour and pour in the water. Mix to a stiff dough and leave in a cool place for 30 minutes.
3. Heat the oil in a saucepan and sauté the onion until soft, about 5 minutes.
4. Mix all the remaining ingredients together and stir in the onion.
5. Divide the pastry into 4 portions and roll out into circles.
6. Place a quarter of the mixture in the centre of each. Dampen the edges and seal to form a pasty shape.

7. Place on a greased baking tray and brush with milk. Bake in the oven at 200°C/400°F/Gas Mark 6 for 15 minutes. Reduce to 160°C/325°F/Gas Mark 3 for a further 15 minutes.

Tomato, Orange and Celery Soup

	Metric	Imperial	American
Makes 4–6 portions			
Grated rind (zest) and juice of 1 orange			
Fresh orange juice from carton	*about 300 ml*	*about ½ pint*	*about 1¼ cups*
Water	*300 ml*	*½ pint*	*1¼ cups*
Corn or sunflower oil	*2 tbsp*	*2 tbsp*	*2 tbsp*
Onions, chopped	*2 medium*	*2 medium*	*2 medium*
Celery stalks, chopped	*4*	*4*	*4*
Canned tomatoes, chopped (with herbs if available)	*397 g*	*14 oz*	*16 oz*
Tomato purée	*1 tsp*	*1 tsp*	*1 tsp*

1. Put juice squeezed from orange in a measuring jug. Make up to 300 ml/½ pint/1¼ cups with orange juice from carton. Add the water.
2. Heat the oil in a large saucepan. Add the onion, celery and orange rind. Stir over a low heat for 5 minutes.
3. Add the tomatoes, tomato purée and the orange juice mixture. Simmer for 15 minutes.
4. This soup is excellent just as it is but, if a thicker soup is preferred, purée all or part of it as desired.

Note: Transport in a wide-necked flask.

Curried Nut Loaf

	Metric	Imperial	American
Makes 6 portions			
Peanuts, ground	*225 g*	*8 oz*	*2 cups*
Wholemeal (whole wheat) breadcrumbs	*225 g*	*8 oz*	*2 cups*
Celery stalks, chopped	*2*	*2*	*2*
Onions, chopped	*2 large*	*2 large*	*2 large*
Peas, fresh or frozen	*50 g*	*2 oz*	*generous ¼ cup*
Ground turmeric	*1 tsp*	*1 tsp*	*1 tsp*
Ground coriander	*1 tsp*	*1 tsp*	*1 tsp*
Ground cumin	*1 tsp*	*1 tsp*	*1 tsp*
Ground ginger	*½ tsp*	*½ tsp*	*½ tsp*
Eggs, beaten	*3*	*3*	*3*
Ground black pepper			

1. In a large mixing bowl combine all the ingredients and mix thoroughly.
2. Press into a 500 g/1 lb loaf tin (7 x 3 inch loaf pan) and cook in the oven at 200°C/400°F/Gas Mark 6 for 30 minutes.
3. When cold, slice into 6 portions. Use one for the lunch box and freeze the rest.

Note: This loaf can be made substituting your favourite herbs for the curry spices.

Pasta and Vegetable Salad

	Metric	Imperial	American
Makes 4 portions			
Wholemeal (whole wheat) pasta shells (leftover pasta can be used)	*225 g*	*8 oz*	*2 cups*
Vegetable oil	*1 tsp*	*1 tsp*	*1 tsp*
Lean chicken, chopped	*175 g*	*6 oz*	*¾ cup*
Cooked peas	*50 g*	*2 oz*	*generous ¼ cup*
Raisins	*50 g*	*2 oz*	*⅓ cup*
Natural yoghurt	*150 ml*	*5 fl oz*	*⅔ cup*
Low fat mayonnaise	*2 tbsp*	*2 tbsp*	*2 tbsp*
Soy sauce	*1 tsp*	*1 tsp*	*1 tsp*
Tomato purée	*1 tsp*	*1 tsp*	*1 tsp*

1. Cook the pasta in a large pan of boiling water until tender, about 10 minutes. Add the 1 teaspoon of oil to prevent sticking. Drain and cool.
2. Mix together the chicken, peas and raisins and combine with the pasta.
3. Beat together the yoghurt, mayonnaise, soy sauce and tomato purée to make the dressing. Pour over the pasta mixture.

German Sausage Sandwich

	Metric	Imperial	American
Makes 2 sandwiches			
Light rye white bread	*4 slices*	*4 slices*	*4 slices*
Vegetable margarine or butter for spreading			
Cabbage, chopped very finely	*2 tbsp*	*2 tbsp*	*2 tbsp*
Eating apples, washed and grated, unpeeled	*2*	*2*	*2*
Juice of ½ lemon			
Fromage frais or mayonnaise (proprietary yoghurt dressings go well with garlic sausage)	*2 tbsp*	*2 tbsp*	*2 tbsp*
Garlic sausage	*8 slices*	*8 slices*	*8 slices*
Ground black pepper			

1. Spread bread with margarine or butter.
2. Mix the cabbage with the apple. Add a few drops of lemon juice and bind together with fromage frais or mayonnaise.
3. On 1 slice of bread place a generous layer of sausage. Folded slices make a more generous filling.
4. Spread a layer of the cabbage and apple mixture on top. Sprinkle with pepper to taste.
5. Add another layer of garlic sausage.
6. Complete the sandwich with another slice of bread.

THE SUMMER TERM

Hopefully the faithful flask can be relegated to the back of the cupboard until September, but with the unpredictability of the weather it is probably a good idea to keep it close to hand just in case a cold spell emerges.

The summer term is the easiest of all to cater for with such a great variety of fruit and vegetables in the shops. However a few days spent planning and freezing before the beginning of term will mean less rush each morning.

Preparing pâtés, dips and fillings for pitta breads and pancakes is the main work for the term. Freeze them in small containers ready to pop straight into the lunch box. We have planned the recipes so that they are interchangeable and can be used to dip crudités, pack a pitta bread or spread a sandwich.

When choosing fruit and vegetables for the term be adventurous and vary the choice from day to day. Take the time to chop up a small pot of fruit salad rather than the same apple a day. Top the fruit with some creamy Greek yoghurt. It is not quite as sharp as ordinary yoghurt but has a lower fat content than cream.

Summer Term

WEEK 1

Monday

Hot Dog Kebab *
Wholemeal (Whole wheat)
  Bread *
Raw Vegetable Sticks
Satchel Snack (page 102)
Apple
Drink

Tuesday

Salami Cucumber Sandwich
Chinese Salad (page 112)
Citrus Yoghurt (page 101)
Peanut Butter Cookies * (page 94)
Drink

Wednesday

Fruit and Cheese Kebab
Wholemeal (Whole wheat) Roll
Muesli Shortbread * (page 95)
Orange
Drink

Thursday

Ben's Beany Salad *
Granary Bread (page 106)
Walnut and Banana Cake *
  (page 92)
Grapes
Drink

Friday

Tuna Medley *
Green Salad (page 114)
Granary Roll (page 106)
Fruit Salad
Drink

* suitable for freezing

Hot Dog Kebabs

	Metric	Imperial	American
Makes 2 kebabs			
Hot dog sausages, cooked	3	3	3
Tomatoes, quartered	2	2	2
Cucumber	5 cm piece	2 inch piece	2 inch piece
Green pepper, deseeded	4 slices	4 slices	4 slices
Pickled onions	2	2	2

1. Slice each sausage into 4.
2. Push alternate pieces of sausage, tomato, cucumber and green pepper onto 2 wooden skewers.
3. Add a pickled onion to the end of each and sprinkle with lemon juice.

Note: These can be prepared the night before, wrapped in foil and stored in the refrigerator.

Salami Cucumber Sandwich

	Metric	Imperial	American
Makes 2 portions			
Eggs, hard-boiled (hard-cooked)	*2*	*2*	*2*
Vegetable margarine	*25 g*	*1 oz*	*2 tbsp*
White or mixed grain bread	*4 slices*	*4 slices*	*4 slices*
Cucumber, sliced	*50 g*	*2 oz*	*2 oz*
Salami, sliced	*50 g*	*2 oz*	*2 oz*

1. Mash the egg with sufficient margarine to form a creamy mixture. Spread on slices of bread. No need to add salt as the salami and margarine contain salt.
2. Place a generous layer of cucumber and salami on the egg.
3. Top up with more egg and complete sandwich with another slice of bread.

Fruit and Cheese Kebabs

	Metric	Imperial	American
Makes 2 kebabs			
Tomatoes, quartered	*2 small*	*2 small*	*2 small*
Eating apple, cut into chunks	*1*	*1*	*1*
Cubes fresh pineapple	*8*	*8*	*8*
Button mushrooms	*4*	*4*	*4*
Low fat hard cheese, cubed	*100 g*	*4 oz*	*¾ cup*
Lemon juice			
Ground black pepper			

Push all the ingredients alternately onto 2 skewers and sprinkle with lemon juice and black pepper.

Note: Any fruits and vegetables in season may be substituted. Wrap in foil to transport.

Ben's Beany Salad

	Metric	Imperial	American
Makes 4 portions			
Cooked red kidney beans	*175 g*	*6 oz*	*1 cup*
Cooked haricot (navy) beans	*175 g*	*6 oz*	*1 cup*
Cooked chick peas	*175 g*	*6 oz*	*1 cup*
Green pepper, deseeded and chopped	*½*	*½*	*½*
Onion, chopped	*1*	*1*	*1*
Sunflower oil	*4 tbsp*	*4 tbsp*	*4 tbsp*
White vinegar	*2 tbsp*	*2 tbsp*	*2 tbsp*
Lemon juice	*1 tbsp*	*1 tbsp*	*1 tbsp*
Tomato purée	*1 tbsp*	*1 tbsp*	*1 tbsp*

1. In a large bowl mix the beans, chick peas, pepper and onion.
2. Beat the oil, vinegar, lemon juice and tomato purée together and use to dress the beans.

Note: This salad can be varied tremendously to taste. Favourite herbs may be added as well as diced raw vegetables. It freezes well, so it is worth making up a large amount and storing in small bags ready for use.

Tuna Medley

	Metric	Imperial	American
Makes 4 portions			
Natural yoghurt	*150 ml*	*5 fl oz*	*⅔ cup*
Low fat mayonnaise	*1 tbsp*	*1 tbsp*	*1 tbsp*
Can tuna fish in brine (drained)	*198 g*	*7 oz*	*7 oz*
Cooked new potatoes, cubed unless tiny	*225 g*	*8 oz*	*1¼ cups*
Cooked French beans, cut into 2.5 cm/1 inch lengths	*225 g*	*8 oz*	*1 cup*
Tomatoes, quartered	*4*	*4*	*4*
Ground black pepper			

1. Mix the yoghurt with the mayonnaise.
2. Combine the tuna fish with the remaining ingredients. Stir in the yoghurt mixture.
3. Serve on a bed of lettuce on the day of use.

Summer Term

Monday	Oliver's Gazpacho * Granary Bread (page 106) Walnut and Banana Cake * (page 92) Peach Drink
Tuesday	Chicken and Walnut Salad Wholemeal (Whole wheat) Bread Carob Bar Apple Drink
Wednesday	Chunky Meat Rolls (page 77) Salad of Choice (page 110) Wholemeal (Whole wheat) Bread Fruity Yoghurt (page 100) Peanut Butter Cookie * (page 94) Drink
Thursday	Peanut Dip * (page 75) Pitta Bread * Raw Vegetable Sticks Summer Fruit Salad Muesli Shortbread * (page 95) Drink
Friday	Sausage and Tomato Roll * (page 76) Granary Bread (page 106) Mark's Munch (page 112) Bar Orange Drink

* suitable for freezing

Oliver's Gazpacho

	Metric	Imperial	American
Makes 4–6 portions			
Green pepper, deseeded and chopped	½	½	½
Piece of cucumber	5 cm	2 inch	2 inch
Onion	1 large	1 large	1 large
Canned tomatoes	750 g	1 lb 12 oz	2 lb
Basil	1 tsp	1 tsp	1 tsp
Oregano	1 tsp	1 tsp	1 tsp
Sunflower oil	2 tbsp	2 tbsp	2 tbsp
Water	450 ml	¾ pint	2 cups
Vegetable or tomato stock (bouillon) cube	1	1	1
Tomato purée	2 tbsp	2 tbsp	2 tbsp

1. Purée the vegetables with the tomatoes in a liquidizer or blender. Stir in the herbs and oil.
2. Mix the water and stock cube with the tomato purée and stir into the gazpacho.
3. Chill in the refrigerator. Serve with wholemeal (whole wheat) bread, chopped cucumber and hard-boiled (hard-cooked) egg.

Note: Transport in a wide-necked flask.

Chicken and Walnut Salad

	Metric	Imperial	American
Makes 4 portions			
Lean cooked chicken, diced	*225 g*	*8 oz*	*1 cup*
Orange, peeled and segmented	*1*	*1*	*1*
Banana, sliced	*1*	*1*	*1*
Walnuts, roughly chopped	*100 g*	*4 oz*	*1 cup*
Natural yoghurt	*150 ml*	*5 fl oz*	*⅔ cup*
Low fat mayonnaise	*1 tbsp*	*1 tbsp*	*1 tbsp*
Ground black pepper			

1. In a bowl combine the chicken, fruit and walnuts.
2. Beat together the yoghurt and mayonnaise.
3. Stir the dressing into the chicken mixture and add pepper to taste.

Peanut Dip

	Metric	Imperial	American
Makes 4 portions			
Skimmed milk	*150 ml*	*¼ pint*	*⅔ cup*
Crunchy peanut butter	*175 g*	*6 oz*	*¾ cup*
Onion, chopped	*1 small*	*1 small*	*1 small*
Soy sauce	*1 tsp*	*1 tsp*	*1 tsp*

1. Blend the milk into the peanut butter (easier if the peanut butter is warmed first).
2. Stir in the onion and soy sauce.
3. Spoon into 4 pots and serve with vegetables cut into sticks.

Sausage and Tomato Rolls

	Metric	Imperial	American
Makes 6 large rolls			
Wholemeal (whole wheat) flour	175 g	6 oz	1½ cups
Baking powder	1½ tsp	1½ tsp	1½ tsp
Vegetable margarine	75 g	3 oz	¼ cup + 2 tbsp
Cold water	6 tbsp	6 tbsp	6 tbsp
Sausage meat	225 g	8 oz	1 cup
Tomatoes, chopped	2	2	2
Tomato purée	1 tbsp	1 tbsp	1 tbsp
Ground black pepper			
Pinch sage (optional)			
Milk to glaze			

1. Sift the flour and baking powder into a large bowl. Rub in the margarine until the mixture resembles breadcrumbs.
2. Stir in the water and mix to form a dough. Cover and leave in a cool place for 20 minutes.
3. Mix the sausage meat, tomatoes, purée and pepper to taste. Add the sage if using.
4. Roll out the pastry to form an oblong and divide into 5 cm/2 inch strips.
5. Place a roll of sausage meat along the length of each. Dampen the edges of the pastry and roll firmly round the sausage. Brush with milk and cut to the desired length.
6. Bake in the oven at 200°C/400°F/Gas Mark 6 for 15 minutes. Reduce the heat to 180°C/350°F/Gas Mark 4 for a further 15 minutes.
7. When cool, freeze and use as required.

Chunky Meat Rolls

	Metric	Imperial	American
Makes 2 rolls			
Cooked sausages	*2*	*2*	*2*
Cucumber, chopped	*1 tbsp*	*1 tbsp*	*1 tbsp*
Prepared mild mustard (optional)	*1 tsp*	*1 tsp*	*1 tsp*
Tomato ketchup	*1 tbsp*	*1 tbsp*	*1 tbsp*
Wholemeal (whole wheat) rolls	*2*	*2*	*2*
Vegetable margarine or butter for spreading			

1. Slice the sausages into small pieces. Stir in the cucumber.
2. Mix together the mustard and ketchup and stir into the sausage and cucumber.
3. Slit open the rolls and spread with margarine or butter.
4. Fill with the sausage mixture.

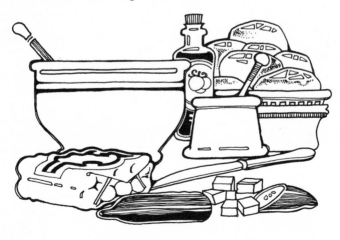

Summary Term

Monday

Cottage Cheese and Chicken
    Spread (page 80)
Wholemeal (Whole wheat) Baps
    or Pitta Bread
Fruit and Nut Nibbles *
    (page 103)
Peach
Drink

Tuesday

Aduki and Rice Salad (page 81)
Wholemeal (Whole wheat) Roll
    (page 105)
Fruit salad
Peanut Butter Cookie * (page 94)
Drink

Wednesday

Taramasalata * (page 80)
Raw Vegetable Sticks
Wholemeal (Whole wheat) Bread
    or Pitta Bread
Walnut and Banana Cake *
    (page 92)
Orange
Drink

Thursday

Pocket Pancakes (Crêpes) *
    (page 79)
Chinese Salad (page 112)
Nutty Yoghurt (page 101)
Nectarine
Drink

Friday

Chunky Cheese Roll (page 82)
Cucumber and Apple Salad
    (page 115)
Satchel Snack (page 102)
Grapes
Drink

* suitable for freezing

Pocket Pancakes (Crêpes)

Wholemeal (whole wheat) pancakes make an interesting alternative to sandwiches and rolls. They may be frozen in batches, defrosted as required and a favourite filling popped in. Use them as a main course or filled with fruit as a dessert. Soft summer fruits are particularly delicious.

To assemble, fold the pancake into quarters to form a pocket to take the filling. This way the school uniform stays cleaner, as the conventional rolled pancake is rather difficult to handle.

BASIC BATTER

Makes 4–6

	Metric	Imperial	American
Wholemeal (whole wheat) flour	*100 g*	*4 oz*	*1 cup*
Eggs, beaten	*2*	*2*	*2*
Skimmed milk	*300 ml*	*½ pint*	*1¼ cups*
Vegetable oil for frying			

1. Place the flour in a large bowl, make a well in the centre and gradually beat in the eggs and milk. Beat to a smooth batter and set aside in the refrigerator for 1 hour.
2. In a small frying pan heat a little oil then pour off any excess.
3. When the oil is hot pour in sufficient batter to cover the base of the pan. Swirl the batter around to cover quickly.
4. When the batter has set flip the pancake over and cook the other side. Do not worry if the first one is not perfect. It takes a while for the pan to reach the right temperature.
5. To freeze interleave the pancakes with greaseproof (waxed) paper and place in a plastic container.

Cottage Cheese and Chicken Spread

	Metric	Imperial	American
Makes 4 portions			
Cottage cheese	*200 g*	*7 oz*	*scant 1 cup*
Canned sweetcorn and red peppers, drained	*200 g*	*7 oz*	*7 oz*
Cold cooked chicken, chopped	*175–225 g*	*6–8 oz*	*¾-1 cup*
Mushrooms	*2 or 3 small*	*2 or 3 small*	*2 or 3 small*
Chives, snipped (chopped)			

1. Mix together all the ingredients.
2. Use as a spread on wholemeal (whole wheat) baps or to fill pitta breads.

Taramasalata

	Metric	Imperial	American
Makes 4–6 portions			
Can smoked cod's roe	*225 g*	*8 oz*	*8 oz*
Wholemeal (whole wheat) bread	*2 slices*	*2 slices*	*2 slices*
Boiled potato	*50 g*	*2 oz*	*¼ cup*
Lemon juice	*3 tbsp*	*3 tbsp*	*3 tbsp*
Chopped parsley	*2 tbsp*	*2 tbsp*	*2 tbsp*
Vinegar	*1 tsp*	*1 tsp*	*1 tsp*
Sunflower or olive oil	*1 tsp*	*1 tsp*	*1 tsp*
Ground black pepper			

1. In a liquidizer or blender combine the cod's roe and bread. Blend until smooth.
2. Add the remaining ingredients and black pepper to taste. Blend again until the smooth consistency returns.
3. Turn into individual pots and freeze, retaining one for use.

Note: This can be served with a selection of raw vegetables or as a filling for pitta bread.

Aduki and Rice Salad

	Metric	Imperial	American
Makes 4 portions			
Cooked brown rice	*350 g*	*12 oz*	*generous 2 cups*
Cooked aduki beans	*100 g*	*4 oz*	*⅔ cup*
Onion, chopped	*1 small*	*1 small*	*1 small*
Carrot, chopped	*1*	*1*	*1*
Apple, chopped	*1*	*1*	*1*
Vegetable oil	*3 tbsp*	*3 tbsp*	*3 tbsp*
Vinegar	*1½ tbsp*	*1½ tbsp*	*1½ tbsp*
Lemon juice	*1 tsp*	*1 tsp*	*1 tsp*
Ground black pepper			
Eggs, hard-boiled (hard-cooked) and sliced	*2*	*2*	*2*

1. In a large bowl mix the rice and beans. Stir in the onion, carrot and apple.
2. Beat together the oil, vinegar, lemon juice and pepper to taste. Use to dress the salad.
3. Garnish with the sliced egg.

Chunky Cheese Rolls

	Metric	Imperial	American
Makes 4 rolls			
Cheddar cheese, grated	*225 g*	*8 oz*	*2 cups*
Raisins	*25 g*	*1 oz*	*3 tbsp*
Celery, chopped	*25 g*	*1 oz*	*¼ cup*
Prepared mild mustard (optional)	*½ tsp*	*½ tsp*	*½ tsp*
Milk	*3–4 tbsp*	*3–4 tbsp*	*3–4 tbsp*
Wholemeal (whole wheat) rolls	*4*	*4*	*4*
Vegetable margarine or butter for spreading			
Tomatoes, sliced	*2*	*2*	*2*

1. Mix together the cheese, raisins and celery.
2. Blend the mustard with the milk and pour into the cheese mixture.
3. Slit open the rolls and spread with margarine or butter.
4. Fill with the cheese mixture topped with tomato slices.

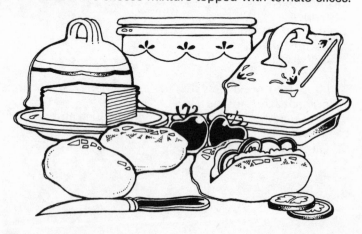

Summer Term

WEEK 4

Monday	Dutch Dinner Sandwich (page 86) Walnut and Banana Cake * (page 92) Strawberries Drink
Tuesday	Peanut and Rice Salad (page 85) Granary Bread (page 106) Fruity Yoghurt (page 100) Drink
Wednesday	Summer Pizza * (page 84) Sweet and Crunchy Cauliflower (page 111) Summer Fruit Salad Peanut Butter Cookie * (page 94) Drink
Thursday	Hungry Haricot Salad * (page 87) Wholemeal (Whole wheat) roll Satchel Snack (page 102) Peach Drink
Friday	Apple and Bacon Sandwich (page 88) Nutty Yoghurt (page 101) Muesli Shortbread * (page 95) or Piece of Fruit Drink

*suitable for freezing

Summer Pizza

	Metric	Imperial	American
Makes 4 × 15 cm/6 inch pizzas			
Wholemeal (whole wheat) flour	*450 g*	*1 lb*	*4 cups*
Easy bake dried yeast	*1 pkt*	*1 pkt*	*1 pkt*
Brown sugar	*1 tsp*	*1 tsp*	*1 tsp*
Egg, beaten	*1*	*1*	*1*
Sunflower oil	*150 ml*	*¼ pint*	*⅔ cup*
Warm water	*about 400 ml*	*about ⅔ pint*	*about 1¾ cups*
TOPPING			
Vegetable oil	*2 tbsp*	*2 tbsp*	*2 tbsp*
Onion, chopped	*1*	*1*	*1*
Red pepper, chopped	*½*	*½*	*½*
Tomato purée	*2 tbsp*	*2 tbsp*	*2 tbsp*
Canned tomatoes	*397 g*	*14 oz*	*16 oz*
Cucumber, diced	*2 tbsp*	*2 tbsp*	*2 tbsp*
Cooked green beans, cut into small slices	*50 g*	*2 oz*	*¼ cup*
Oregano	*½ tsp*	*½ tsp*	*½ tsp*
Basil	*½ tsp*	*½ tsp*	*½ tsp*
Ground black pepper			
Tomatoes, sliced	*4*	*4*	*4*
Cheese, grated	*75 g*	*3 oz*	*¾ cup*

1. Place the flour in a large bowl and stir in the yeast and sugar.
2. Mix the egg with the oil and add sufficient water to make up to 400 ml/⅔ pint/1¾ cups. Pour in the liquid and stir to form a dough.
3. Gather the dough together using your hands and knead on a floured board for 10 minutes (a marvellous job to delegate).

4. Cut the dough into 4 equal portions and roll out to form pizzas about 5 mm/¼ inch thick.
5. Cover with a polythene (plastic) bag and leave in a warm place to rise, about 30 minutes.
6. Meanwhile, heat the 2 tablespoons oil in a saucepan and sauté the onion until just turning transparent, about 5 minutes. Add the red pepper and cook for a further 3 minutes.
7. Stir in the tomato purée and canned tomatoes. Simmer until the mixture forms a pulp. Stir in the cucumber and beans, oregano, basil and black pepper to taste.
8. Spoon sauce over the pizza bases and arrange the tomatoes on top. Sprinkle over the cheese. Bake in the oven at 220°C/425°F/Gas Mark 7 for 12–15 minutes.

Note: These pizzas freeze well.

Peanut and Rice Salad

	Metric	Imperial	American
Makes 2 portions			
Curry powder (optional)	*½ tsp*	*½ tsp*	*½ tsp*
Natural yoghurt	*2 tbsp*	*2 tbsp*	*2 tbsp*
Cooked brown rice	*100 g*	*4 oz*	*¾ cup*
Onion, chopped	*½ small*	*½ small*	*½ small*
Celery stalks, chopped	*2*	*2*	*2*
Carrot, diced	*1*	*1*	*1*
Roasted peanuts	*25 g*	*1 oz*	*¼ cup*

1. If using the curry powder mix it with the yoghurt.
2. Mix the rice, vegetables and nuts together. Dress with the yoghurt.

Note: This is a good way to use leftover rice and vegetables. Vary the recipe using favourite vegetables in season.

Dutch Dinner Sandwich

	Metric	Imperial	American
Makes 2 sandwiches			
Carrots, grated	*2 medium*	*2 medium*	*2 medium*
Raisins, soaked in cold tea, orange juice or warm water	*50 g*	*2 oz*	*⅓ cup*
Mayonnaise, yoghurt or fromage frais	*2 tbsp*	*2 tbsp*	*2 tbsp*
Sunflower or soya margarine for spreading			
Mixed grain or granary bread	*4 slices*	*4 slices*	*4 slices*
Dutch sausage, skinned and sliced	*1*	*1*	*1*

1. Mix together the carrot, soaked raisins and mayonnaise, yoghurt or fromage frais. The mixture should bind together but should not be so moist as to make the bread soggy.
2. Spread the bread with margarine. Top 2 slices with the carrot mixture and sausage. Add another layer of carrot mixture and slices of bread to complete the sandwich.

Hungry Haricot Salad

	Metric	Imperial	American
Makes 4 portions			
Cooked haricot beans	225 g	8 oz	1⅓ cups
Onion, chopped	1	1	1
Green pepper, deseeded and chopped	½	½	½
Red pepper, deseeded and chopped	½	½	½
Mushrooms, sliced	50 g	2 oz	½ cup
Natural yoghurt	150 ml	5 fl oz	⅔ cup
Low fat mayonnaise	2 tbsp	2 tbsp	2 tbsp
Basil	1 tsp	1 tsp	1 tsp
Oregano	1 tsp	1 tsp	1 tsp
Ground black pepper			

1. Combine the beans, onion, peppers and mushrooms.
2. Beat together the yoghurt, mayonnaise and herbs. Add pepper to taste. Use to dress the beans.

Note: This is equally good using a French dressing instead of the yoghurt and mayonnaise.

Apple and Bacon Sandwich

	Metric	Imperial	American
Makes 2 sandwiches			
Light rye or caraway seed bread	*4 slices*	*4 slices*	*4 slices*
Sunflower or vegetable margarine for spreading			
Chopped meat from cooked hock or shoulder bacon	*100 g*	*4 oz*	*½ cup*
Eating apples (unpeeled), grated	*2*	*2*	*2*
Juice of lemon	*½*	*½*	*½*
Ground black pepper			

1. Spread the bread with margarine.
2. Cover half the slices with a generous layer of meat.
3. Add a layer of the grated apple. Sprinkle with lemon juice and black pepper to taste.
4. Top with another layer of meat.
5. Sandwich together with remaining slices of bread.

ALTERNATIVE PUDDINGS

Ultimately we would hope that every lunch box meal would end with a spoonful of natural sugar, i.e. a piece of fruit. However just as babies need to be weaned from milk so does the sweet tooth require to go through a weaning process. To facilitate this the following recipes have been included because they are comparatively low in fat and sugar and high in fibre.

Gingerbread

Quick Mix Fruit Cake

Fruity Compote

Walnut and Banana Cake

Carrot Cake

Peanut Butter Cookies

Fruit Scones

Muesli Shortbread

Fruity Bread Pudding

Apple Crunch

Carob Brownies

Bran Fruit Loaf

Apricot Slice

Fruity Yoghurt

Summer Fruit Yoghurt

Citrus Yoghurt

Nutty Yoghurt

Winter Fruit Salad

Satchel Snack

Fruit and Nut Nibbles

Nutty Crunchies

Gingerbread

	Metric	Imperial	American
Makes 8 slices			
Hard vegetable margarine	100 g	4 oz	½ cup
Molasses	175 g	6 oz	½ cup
Golden syrup (corn syrup)	50 g	2 oz	3 tbsp
Skimmed milk	150 ml	¼ pint	⅔ cup
Eggs, beaten	2	2	2
Plain flour, half wholemeal (all-purpose flour, half whole wheat)	225 g	8 oz	2 cups
Brown raw cane sugar	50 g	2 oz	⅓ cup
Mixed spice	1 tsp	1 tsp	1 tsp
Ground ginger	2 tsp	2 tsp	2 tsp
Bicarbonate of soda (baking soda)	1 tsp	1 tsp	1 tsp

1. In a medium sized saucepan warm together the margarine, molasses and golden syrup. Take care not to overheat.
2. Add the milk, allow to cool. Stir in the eggs.
3. In a separate bowl mix together the flour, sugar, spices and bicarbonate of soda.
4. Add the dry ingredients to the cooled mixture in the pan. Stir well.
5. Pour the mixture (batter) into a greased and lined 18 cm/7 inch square tin (baking pan).
6. Bake in the oven at 160°C/325°F/Gas Mark 3 for about 45 minutes or until firm to the touch.

This dark moist gingerbread is always a firm favourite. It is delicious eaten with a soft cheese such as Brie and a crunchy apple or with a handful of sunflower seeds and some large juicy raisins.

Quick Mix Fruit Cake

	Metric	Imperial	American
Makes 8 slices			
Self-raising flour, half wholemeal (self-rising flour, half whole wheat)	*225 g*	*8 oz*	*2 cups*
Baking powder	*1 tsp*	*1 tsp*	*1 tsp*
Mixed spice	*2 tsp*	*2 tsp*	*2 tsp*
Soft vegetable margarine	*100 g*	*4 oz*	*½ cup*
Brown sugar	*100 g*	*4 oz*	*⅔ cup*
Milk	*1 tbsp*	*1 tbsp*	*1 tbsp*
Eggs	*2*	*2*	*2*
Mixed dried fruit	*225 g*	*8 oz*	*1⅓ cups*
Chopped (candied) peel	*25 g*	*1 oz*	*3 tbsp*
Glacé (candied) cherries	*25 g*	*1 oz*	*2 tbsp*
Chopped walnuts	*25 g*	*1 oz*	*¼ cup*

1. In a large bowl, combine flour with baking powder and spice.
2. Add remaining ingredients and mix well.
3. Pour the mixture into a greased and lined 20 cm/ 8 inch cake tin (baking pan).
4. Bake in the oven at 160°C/325°F/Gas Mark 3 for about 1¼ hours.

Fruity Compote

	Metric	Imperial	American
Makes 4 portions			
Dried apricots	*100 g*	*4 oz*	*⅔ cup*
Dried prunes	*100 g*	*4 oz*	*⅔ cup*
Raisins	*100 g*	*4 oz*	*⅔ cup*
Sultanas (golden raisins)	*100 g*	*4 oz*	*⅔ cup*
Dried apple rings	*100 g*	*4 oz*	*¼ lb*
Apple juice	*300 ml*	*½ pint*	*1¼ cups*

1. Soak all the fruit in the apple juice overnight.
2. Place the fruit and juice in a saucepan, bring to the boil and simmer gently for 15 minutes. Alternatively, cook the compote in a microwave for 5 minutes.
3. Divide into 4 containers.

Walnut and Banana Cake

	Metric	Imperial	American
Makes 8 slices			
Vegetable margarine	*50 g*	*2 oz*	*¼ cup*
Brown sugar	*75 g*	*3 oz*	*½ cup*
Eggs	*3*	*3*	*3*
Bananas, mashed	*3 large*	*3 large*	*3 large*
Wholemeal self-raising flour (whole wheat self-rising flour)	*225 g*	*8 oz*	*2 cups*
Walnuts, chopped	*175 g*	*6 oz*	*1½ cups*

1. In a bowl, cream the margarine and sugar together until smooth.
2. Beat in the eggs one at a time until the mixture is fluffy and light.
3. Beat in the bananas.

4. Stir in the flour and walnuts and beat well.
5. Pour into a greased 500 g/1 lb loaf tin (7 × 3 inch loaf pan) and bake in the oven at 180°C/350°F/Gas Mark 4 for 55 minutes.

Note: When cool the cake can be sliced into portions and frozen.

Carrot Cake

	Metric	Imperial	American
Makes 8 slices			
Wholemeal self-raising (whole wheat self-rising) flour	*225 g*	*8 oz*	*2 cups*
Baking powder	*2 level tsp*	*2 level tsp*	*2 level tsp*
Carrot, finely chopped	*100 g*	*4 oz*	*1 cup*
Bananas, mashed	*2*	*2*	*2*
Eggs	*2*	*2*	*2*
Walnuts, chopped	*50 g*	*2 oz*	*½ cup*
Brown sugar	*100 g*	*4 oz*	*⅔ cup*
Ground cinnamon	*2 tsp*	*2 tsp*	*2 tsp*
Vanilla essence (extract)	*1 tsp*	*1 tsp*	*1 tsp*
Corn oil	*150 ml*	*¼ pint*	*⅔ cup*

1. Mix all the ingredients together in a large bowl until combined. Pour into a greased 500 g/1 lb loaf tin (7 × 3 inch loaf pan).
2. Bake in the oven at 180°C/350°F/Gas Mark 4 for 1¼ hours.

Peanut Butter Cookies

	Metric	Imperial	American
Makes 10 cookies			
Crunchy peanut butter	2 tbsp	2 tbsp	2 tbsp
Vegetable margarine	65 g	2½ oz	¼ cup + 1 tbsp
Wholemeal plain (whole wheat all-purpose) flour	150 g	5 oz	1¼ cups
Water	2 tbsp	2 tbsp	2 tbsp

1. In a saucepan melt the peanut butter and margarine together over a gentle heat. Mix in the flour.
2. Make a well in the centre and stir in the water. Mix to make a firm dough.
3. Divide into 10 equal portions and flatten to about 5 mm/¼ inch thick.
4. Place on a greased tray and bake in the oven at 180°C/350°F/Gas Mark 4 for 20 minutes.

Fruit Scones

	Metric	Imperial	American
Makes 16 scones			
Vegetable margarine	175 g	6 oz	¾ cup
Wholemeal self-raising flour (whole wheat self-rising flour)	450 g	1 lb	4 cups
Brown sugar	50 g	2 oz	⅓ cup
Sultanas (golden raisins	150 g	5 oz	scant 1 cup
Skimmed milk	250 ml	8 fl oz	1 cup

1. In a large bowl, rub the margarine into the flour until the mixture resembles breadcrumbs. Stir in the sugar and sultanas.
2. Make a well in the centre and pour in the milk. Mix to form a soft dough.
3. Knead lightly on a floured board and roll out to a thickness of 1.5–2.5 cm/¾–1 inch. Using a 5 cm/2 inch fluted cutter cut out the scones and place on a lightly greased baking sheet.
4. Bake in the oven at 220°C/425°F/Gas Mark 7 for 10 minutes until well-risen and golden brown.

Note: When cool these freeze well and can be added to the lunch box as required.

Muesli Shortbread

	Metric	Imperial	American
Makes 12 biscuits			
Vegetable margarine	150 g	5 oz	½ cup + 2 tbsp
Wholemeal plain flour (whole wheat all-purpose flour)	175 g	6 oz	1½ cups
Brown sugar	50 g	2 oz	⅓ cup
Muesli (granola) with no added sugar	75 g	3 oz	1 cup

1. Rub the margarine into the flour until the mixture resembles fine breadcrumbs.
2. Stir in the sugar and muesli and knead to form a stiff paste. This may take a while depending on the room temperature but it will eventually hold together.
3. Press into a shortbread mould or form a neat shape on a greased baking sheet.
4. Bake in the oven at 160°C/325°F/Gas Mark 3 for 20–30 minutes, until golden brown.
5. When cool store in an airtight container.

Fruity Bread Pudding

	Metric	Imperial	American
Serves 6			
Wholemeal (whole wheat) bread, thinly sliced	*12 slices*	*12 slices*	*12 slices*
Mixed spice	*1 tsp*	*1 tsp*	*1 tsp*
Mixed dried fruit or dates and nuts	*175 g*	*6 oz*	*1 cup*
Orange juice	*2 tbsp*	*2 tbsp*	*2 tbsp*
Grated orange rind (zest) (optional)			
Egg, beaten	*1*	*1*	*1*
Raw cane sugar for topping	*sprinkling*	*sprinkling*	*sprinkling*

1. Remove the crusts from the bread, then cut the bread into pieces. Place in a bowl and moisten with a little water or milk to make a soggy mixture. Leave to soak for 10 minutes.
2. Mix the spice into the dried fruit and moisten with the orange juice. Add the orange rind if using.
3. Mash the wet bread with a fork. Add the fruit mixture and egg to the bread, stirring well.
4. Turn the mixture into a greased 19 cm/7½ inch oven-proof soufflé dish.
5. Bake in the oven at 160°C/325°F/Gas Mark 3 until top of the pudding is set, about 35 minutes. Remove from oven and sprinkle with sugar. Return to oven to complete cooking, about 10 minutes.
6. Remove from oven and run knife around the edge when still warm in the dish.

Apple Crunch

	Metric	Imperial	American
Makes 4 portions			
Cooking (tart) apples, sliced	450 g	1 lb	4 cups
Water	2 tbsp	2 tbsp	2 tbsp
Brown sugar	75 g	3 oz	½ cup
Ground cinnamon	½ tsp	½ tsp	½ tsp
Vegetable margarine	75 g	3 oz	¼ cup + 2 tbsp
Wholemeal plain (whole wheat all-purpose) flour	100 g	4 oz	1 cup
Oat flakes	50 g	2 oz	⅔ cup
Sesame seeds	2 tsp	2 tsp	2 tsp

1. Cook the apples in the water with half the sugar and the cinnamon until just soft. Divide between 4 small ovenproof containers.
2. Rub the margarine into the flour until the mixture resembles breadcrumbs. Stir in the remaining sugar, oat flakes and sesame seeds.
3. Spread evenly over the apple. Bake in the oven at 220°C/425°F/Gas Mark 7 for 20 minutes.

Carob Brownies

	Metric	Imperial	American
Makes 12			
Wholemeal self-raising flour (whole wheat self-rising flour)	*100 g*	*4 oz*	*1 cup*
Brown sugar	*100 g*	*4 oz*	*⅔ cup*
Carob powder	*50 g*	*2 oz*	*½ cup*
Sultanas (golden raisins)	*50 g*	*2 oz*	*⅓ cup*
Egg, beaten	*1*	*1*	*1*
Skimmed milk	*150 ml*	*¼ pint*	*⅔ cup*

1. Mix all the dry ingredients in a bowl, ensuring that there are no lumps in the carob. Stir in the sultanas.
2. Add the egg and milk stirring well.
3. Pour the mixture into a greased bun tray.
4. Bake in the oven at 160°C/325°F/Gas Mark 3 for about 20 minutes.

Note: For a change, 50 g/2 oz/½ cup chopped walnuts may be substituted for the sultanas.

Bran Fruit Loaf

	Metric	Imperial	American
Makes 1 loaf			
All-Bran	*100 g*	*4 oz*	*generous 1½ cups*
Raw cane sugar	*75 g*	*3 oz*	*½ cup*
Mixed dried fruit	*175 g*	*6 oz*	*1 cup*
Milk	*280 ml*	*9 fl oz*	*generous 1 cup*
85% self-raising (self-rising) flour	*100 g*	*4 oz*	*1 cup*

1. Place All-Bran, sugar and dried fruit in a bowl, mix well. Stir in the milk and leave to stand for at least 1 hour.
2. Mix in the flour. Put mixture into a greased 1 kg/2 lb loaf tin (9 × 5 inch loaf pan).
3. Bake in the oven at 160°C/325°F/Gas Mark 3 for about 1 hour.

Apricot Slice

	Metric	Imperial	American
Makes 12–16 slices			
Dried apricots	*225 g*	*8 oz*	*1⅓ cups*
Water	*2 tbsp*	*2 tbsp*	*2 tbsp*
Concentrated apple juice	*2 tbsp*	*2 tbsp*	*2 tbsp*
Brown sugar	*100 g*	*4 oz*	*⅔ cup*
Vegetable margarine	*150 g*	*5 oz*	*½ cup + 2 tbsp*
Porridge oats	*225 g*	*8 oz*	*generous 2 cups*

1. Soak the apricots overnight in the water and apple juice. Alternatively heat in a microwave until softened.
2. Purée the apricots in a blender or liquidizer with the soaking liquid.
3. In a saucepan heat the sugar and margarine until melted. Stir in the oats.
4. Press half the oat mixture into the base of a greased 20 cm/8 inch cake tin (baking pan). Pour in the apricot sauce and spread evenly.
5. Press the remaining oats on top. Bake in the oven at 180°C/350°F/Gas Mark 4 for 50 minutes or until browned.
6. Cut into slices and leave to cool in the tin.

Note: The slices can be frozen.

Fruity Yoghurt

	Metric	Imperial	American
Makes 4 pots			
Natural yoghurt	*300 ml*	*½ pint*	*1¼ cups*
Raisins	*25 g*	*1 oz*	*3 tbsp*
Sultanas (golden raisins)	*25 g*	*1 oz*	*3 tbsp*
Desiccated (shredded) coconut	*1 tbsp*	*1 tbsp*	*1 tbsp*
Dried apricots, chopped	*25 g*	*1 oz*	*3 tbsp*

1. Mix all the ingredients together and refrigerate overnight.
2. Transfer to small pots.

Summer Fruit Yoghurt

	Metric	Imperial	American
Makes 4 pots			
Natural yoghurt	*300 ml*	*½ pint*	*1¼ cups*
Mixed berries (raspberries, blackcurrants, redcurrants)	*100 g*	*4 oz*	*1 cup*
Sunflower seeds	*25 g*	*1 oz*	*¼ cup*

1. Mix all the ingredients together and refrigerate overnight.
2. Transfer to 4 small pots.

Citrus Yoghurt

	Metric	Imperial	American
Makes 4 pots			
Natural yoghurt	300 ml	½ pint	1¼ cups
Orange, chopped	1	1	1
Grapefruit, chopped	½	½	½
Grated orange rind (zest)	1 tsp	1 tsp	1 tsp
Grated lemon rind	1 tsp	1 tsp	1 tsp

1. Mix all the ingredients together and refrigerate overnight.
2. Transfer to 4 small pots.

Note: This may require the addition of a little brown sugar. Attempt to reduce this as the child becomes accustomed to the tangy flavour of the fruit.

Nutty Yoghurt

	Metric	Imperial	American
Makes 4 pots			
Natural yoghurt	300 ml	½ pint	1¼ cups
Hazelnuts, chopped	25 g	1 oz	¼ cup
Walnuts, chopped	25 g	1 oz	¼ cup
Sweet apple, chopped	1 small	1 small	1 small

1. Mix all the ingredients together and refrigerate overnight.
2. Transfer to 4 small pots.

Winter Fruit Salad

Any variations of fruit may be used to make a fruit salad. The following are suggestions only.

Apple, banana, oranges (fresh or canned), cucumber. Pour over unsweetened pineapple juice from a carton.

Satsumas, melon, kiwi fruit, unpeeled red-skinned apples. Sprinkle on a few walnuts. Pour over fresh unsweetened orange juice.

Banana, apples, pineapple (canned or preferably fresh), grapes. Pour over unsweetened pineapple juice from a carton.

Satchel Snack

A packet of this snack is the best alternative there is to sticky sweets. Make up a batch of 20 bags and they will remain quite fresh for the 4 week cycle.

	Metric	Imperial	American
Makes 5 bags			
Flaked coconut	*100 g*	*4 oz*	*¼ lb*
Hazelnuts	*50 g*	*2 oz*	*generous ¼ cup*
Sunflower seeds	*50 g*	*2 oz*	*½ cup*
Dried pineapple	*50 g*	*2 oz*	*⅓ cup*
Dried apricots	*50 g*	*2 oz*	*⅓ cup*
Dried banana (honey dipped)	*50 g*	*2 oz*	*3 tbsp*
Sultanas (golden raisins)	*50 g*	*2 oz*	*⅓ cup*
Raisins	*50 g*	*2 oz*	*⅓ cup*
Currants	*50 g*	*2 oz*	*⅓ cup*

1. Mix all the ingredients together in a bowl.
2. Divide into 5 polythene (plastic) bags and store in a cool place to use as required.

Fruit and Nut Nibbles

	Metric	Imperial	American
Dried apricots	50 g	2 oz	⅓ cup
Sultanas (golden raisins)	50 g	2 oz	⅓ cup
Raisins	50 g	2 oz	⅓ cup
Dried apple	50 g	2 oz	⅓ cup
Dried prunes, stoned	50 g	2 oz	⅓ cup
Hazelnuts, chopped	50 g	2 oz	½ cup
Sunflower seeds	50 g	2 oz	½ cup
Desiccated (shredded) coconut	50 g	2 oz	⅔ cup

1. Put all the dried fruit through a mincer or liquidizer.
2. Stir in the hazelnuts and seeds.
3. Form into balls and roll in the desiccated coconut. Store in an airtight container.

Nutty Crunchies

	Metric	Imperial	American
Breakfast cereal, no added sugar	225 g	8 oz	8 oz
Mixed nuts, chopped	100 g	4 oz	1 cup
Vegetable margarine	50 g	2 oz	¼ cup

1. Mix all the ingredients together.
2. Form into balls and place on a greased baking tray. Bake in the oven at 160°C/325°F/Gas Mark 3. Cool and store in an airtight container.

BREAD AND SCONES

Home bread making is rapidly increasing in popularity, largely due to the fact that we now realise that a high fibre diet is essential for health. Home baked brown wholemeal (whole wheat) and granary bread is a delicious source of that necessary fibre.

This revival of an ancient skill also owes something to the introduction of the new easy mix dry yeast and the greater availability of a whole range of bread flours suitable for home baking.

If you have never made bread try our easy recipes, save money and ensure your family are getting high fibre bread, low in salt and without additives.

Bread freezes well, so batch baking loaves, pizza bases, bread buns and pitta bread ensures that you are always able to produce a nutritionally sound and appetising meal at a moment's notice.

Savoury scones provide a wholesome alternative to serve with soups. Variety may be obtained by the addition of favourite herbs and spices.

Wholemeal Bread

	Metric	Imperial	American
Makes 4 loaves			
Wholemeal (whole wheat) bread flour	*1.5 kg*	*3 lb*	*12 cups*
Salt	*15–25 g*	*½–1 oz*	*1–2 tbsp*
Easy bake dried yeast	*1–2 sachets*	*1–2 sachets*	*1–2 sachets*
Raw cane sugar	*25 g*	*1 oz*	*2 tbsp*
Sunflower or corn oil	*2 tbsp*	*2 tbsp*	*2 tbsp*
Lukewarm water	*900 ml*	*1½ pints*	*3¾ cups*

1. Mix together the flour, salt and yeast in a large bowl. Add the sugar.
2. Mix the oil with the water. Gradually pour the water and oil into the dry ingredients, using a large spoon. Work the flour in well until a soft but not sticky dough.
3. Turn out the dough onto a floured board and knead for 10 minutes until the dough is elastic.
4. Shape into a ball and put into an oiled bowl, cover with oiled polythene (plastic) or a clean damp cloth. Leave to prove for 1 hour in a warm place.
5. Transfer the dough to floured board and knead very lightly. Cut and shape into 4 pieces to fit 500 g/1 lb bread tins (7 × 3 inch loaf pans) or shape into flat loaves. Alternatively, roll into small balls for rolls and place on baking sheets.
6. Cover and leave to prove again for about 20 minutes or until the loaves rise to the top of the tins.
7. Bake in the oven at 230°C/450°F/Gas Mark 8 for 40 minutes.
8. Turn out and cool on a wire rack.

Note: If 100% wholemeal seems rather too solid, try mixing strong white flour and granary flour with the wholemeal. Look out for special flours that contain ingredients such as poppy seeds and sesame seeds, or try adding your own. For quantity of easy bake, dried yeast, follow manufacturers instructions.

Granary Bread

	Metric	Imperial	American
Makes 4 loaves			
Easy bake dried yeast	*2 sachets*	*2 sachets*	*2 sachets*
Salt	*3 tsp*	*3 tsp*	*3 tsp*
Raw cane sugar	*2 tsp*	*2 tsp*	*2 tsp*
Granary (whole wheat) flour	*1.5 kg*	*3 lb*	*12 cups*
Sunflower or corn oil	*2 tbsp*	*2 tbsp*	*2 tbsp*
Warm water or milk and water mixed	*900 ml*	*1½ pints*	*3¾ cups*
Milk for glazing (optional)	*2 tbsp*	*2 tbsp*	*2 tbsp*
Sunflower seeds (optional)	*50 g*	*2 oz*	*3 tbsp*

1. Stir the yeast, salt and sugar into the flour in a large bowl.
2. Add the oil and warm liquid and combine. Knead thoroughly for 10 minutes on a floured board.
3. Cut and shape into 4 loaves. Place in well oiled 500 g/ 1 lb bread tins (7 × 3 inch loaf pans). Alternatively, roll into small balls for rolls and place on baking sheets.
4. Cover and leave in a warm place to prove. When the loaves or rolls are well risen and doubled in size, they are ready for baking.
5. If you wish to glaze the bread, brush with milk and, if liked, sprinkle with sunflower seeds.
6. Bake in the oven at 200–220°C/400–425°F/Gas Mark 6–7 for 35 minutes.
7. Turn out onto a wire rack to cool.

Note: The warm liquid may be made up from a mixture of skimmed milk and water in any proportion. A beaten egg may be added to the liquid for a more enriched dough.

Onion Scones

	Metric	Imperial	American
Makes 12			
Sunflower oil	*2 tbsp*	*2 tbsp*	*2 tbsp*
Onion, chopped	*1*	*1*	*1*
Vegetable margarine	*175 g*	*6 oz*	*¾ cup*
Wholemeal self-raising (whole wheat self-rising) flour	*450 g*	*1 lb*	*4 cups*
Skimmed milk	*250 ml*	*8 fl oz*	*1 cup*
Ground black pepper			

1. Heat the oil in a saucepan and sauté the onion until soft.
2. Rub the margarine into the flour until the mixture resembles fine breadcrumbs.
3. Make a well in the centre and stir in the onion, milk and pepper to taste. Stir gently until all the flour has been incorporated.
4. Turn onto a floured board and roll out to 1.5 cm/¾ inch thickness. Cut out rounds with a fluted scone cutter and place on a greased baking tray.
5. Bake in the oven at 220°C/425°F/Gas Mark 7 for 12 minutes until golden.

Note: These make a pleasant change from bread to accompany a hearty soup or stew.

Cheese Scones

	Metric	Imperial	American
Makes 8–10 scones			
Self-raising (self-rising) flour	225 g	8 oz	2 cups
Salt (optional)	½ tsp	½ tsp	½ tsp
Margarine	50 g	2 oz	¼ cup
Cheese, grated	75 g	3 oz	¾ cup
Cayenne pepper	pinch	pinch	pinch
Milk	150 ml	¼ pint	⅔ cup

1. Mix flour and salt together. Rub in the margarine, until mixture resembles breadcrumbs.
2. Stir in the cheese and the pepper.
3. Add the milk and mix to a soft dough.
4. Turn onto a lightly floured board. Press mixture with the hands, handle lightly. When spread out to a thickness of about 2.5 cm/1 inch cut into rounds with a fluted scone cutter.
5. Place on a floured baking sheet. Bake in the oven at 230°C/450°F/Gas Mark 8 for about 15 minutes.

Potato Scones

	Metric	Imperial	American
Makes 8 scones			
Butter	50 g	2 oz	¼ cup
Cooked mashed potato	350 g	12 oz	1½ cups
Self-raising (self-rising) flour	75 g	3 oz	¾ cup
Salt	scant ¼ tsp	scant ¼ tsp	scant ¼ tsp
A little cheese, grated (optional)			

1. Melt butter in a saucepan and stir in the mashed potato. Add flour, salt and cheese, if using, and mix well.
2. Roll out on a floured board to 1 cm/½ inch thickness and cut into rounds with a fluted scone cutter.
3. Place on floured baking sheet and bake in the oven at 200°C/400°F/Gas Mark 6 for 10-15 minutes.
4. Split and spread with margarine, savoury vegetable spread or Marmite. Potato scones are also good eaten with soups.

Corn Muffins

	Metric	Imperial	American
Makes 8			
Wholemeal plain (whole wheat all-purpose) flour	100 g	4 oz	1 cup
Cornmeal	75 g	3 oz	⅔ cup
Baking powder	2 tsp	2 tsp	2 tsp
Egg	1	1	1
Skimmed milk	150 ml	¼ pint	⅔ cup
Honey	1 tbsp	1 tbsp	1 tbsp
Cheese, grated (optional)	50 g	2 oz	½ cup

1. In a large bowl mix together all the dry ingredients.
2. Whisk together the egg, milk and honey. Pour the liquid onto the flour and beat well. Stir in the cheese if used.
3. Spoon the batter into a greased bun tray (muffin pan) and bake in the oven at 200°C/400°F/Gas Mark 6 for 10 minutes until golden.

Note: For extra flavour add 1 teaspoon mixed herbs.

SALADS

Herby Potatoes

	Metric	Imperial	American
Makes 4 portions			
New potatoes	*450 g*	*1 lb*	*2⅔ cups*
Low fat			
mayonnaise	*2 tsp*	*2 tsp*	*2 tsp*
Natural yoghurt	*150 ml*	*5 fl oz*	*⅔ cup*
Onion, chopped	*1 small*	*1 small*	*1 small*
Chives, snipped	*2 tsp*	*2 tsp*	*2 tsp*
Mint, chopped	*1 tsp*	*1 tsp*	*1 tsp*

1. Cook the potatoes in their skins and cut into neat cubes.
2. Beat the mayonnaise into the yoghurt.
3. When the potatoes are cold stir in the onion, chives and mint and dress with the yoghurt dressing.

Sweet and Crunchy Cauliflower

	Metric	Imperial	American
Makes 2 portions			
Cauliflower, broken into florets	½ small	½ small	½ small
Dessert apple, chopped	1	1	1
Dates, chopped	25 g	1 oz	3 tbsp
Banana, sliced	1	1	1
Low fat mayonnaise	2 tbsp	2 tbsp	2 tbsp
Lemon juice	1 tbsp	1 tbsp	1 tbsp
Natural yoghurt	4 tbsp	4 tbsp	4 tbsp

1. Mix the cauliflower with the apple, dates and banana.
2. Beat the mayonnaise and lemon juice into the yoghurt and use to dress the cauliflower and fruit.

Rooty Vegetables

	Metric	Imperial	American
Makes 2 portions			
Parsnip, grated	1	1	1
Carrots, grated	2	2	2
Onion, grated	½	½	½
Turnip, grated	small piece	small piece	small piece
Orange, chopped	½	½	½
French dressing to taste			

1. Mix all the vegetables together with the orange.
2. Dress with a little French dressing or as desired.

Chinese Salad

Bean sprouts are now widely available in supermarkets and health food shops and are a cheap addition to the packed lunch. They are extremely nutritious and great fun to grow at home.

	Metric	Imperial	American
Makes 2 portions			
Fresh orange juice	*1 tbsp*	*1 tbsp*	*1 tbsp*
Lemon juice	*1 tsp*	*1 tsp*	*1 tsp*
Soy sauce	*1 tsp*	*1 tsp*	*1 tsp*
Orange, cubed	*1*	*1*	*1*
Bean sprouts	*75–100 g*	*3–4 oz*	*¾–1 cup*
Cucumber, diced	*5 cm piece*	*2 inch piece*	*2 inch piece*

1. Beat together the fruit juices and soy sauce.
2. Mix the cubed orange, bean sprouts and cucumber together and dress with the fruit juices.

Note: For a main meal add 25 g/1 oz/¼ cup cashew nuts or 25 g/1 oz 2 tablespoons diced chicken or 25 g/1 oz/ 2 tablespoons cubed cheese.

Mark's Munch

	Metric	Imperial	American
Makes 4 portions			
Raisins	*2 tbsp*	*2 tbsp*	*2 tbsp*
Hazelnuts	*2 tbsp*	*2 tbsp*	*2 tbsp*
White cabbage	*½ small*	*½ small*	*½ small*
Carrots, grated	*2*	*2*	*2*
Onion, chopped	*1 small*	*1 small*	*1 small*
Mayonnaise	*2 tsp*	*2 tsp*	*2 tsp*
Natural yoghurt	*150 ml*	*5 fl oz*	*⅔ cup*
Ground black pepper			

1. In a large bowl combine the raisins, hazelnuts and vegetables.
2. Beat the mayonnaise into the yoghurt and use to dress the salad, adding pepper to taste.

Tabouli

	Metric	Imperial	American
Makes 4 portions			
Cracked wheat **(bulgar wheat)**	*175 g*	*6 oz*	*1½ cups*
Olive or **sunflower oil**	*5 tbsp*	*5 tbsp*	*5 tbsp*
Lemon juice	*4 tbsp*	*4 tbsp*	*4 tbsp*
Tomatoes, chopped	*4*	*4*	*4*
Onion, chopped	*1*	*1*	*1*
Chopped parsley	*3 tbsp*	*3 tbsp*	*3 tbsp*
Mint, chopped	*2 tbsp*	*2 tbsp*	*2 tbsp*

1. Soak the wheat in sufficient water to cover for 30 minutes. Drain thoroughly.
2. Whisk the oil and lemon juice together.
3. Mix the wheat, tomatoes, onion and herbs and pour over the dressing.

Note: This is unsuitable for freezing. It is best made the night before you intend to use it to allow the wheat to absorb flavours. Although many young people are unfamiliar with this grain, it is one which they very quickly learn to enjoy.

Green Salad

	Metric	Imperial	American
Makes 2 portions			
Lettuce leaves, shredded (the darker leaves are more nutritious)	*6*	*6*	*6*
Cucumber, diced	*5 cm piece*	*2 inch piece*	*2 inch piece*
Stalk celery, sliced	*1*	*1*	*1*
Green pepper, deseeded and chopped	*1 tbsp*	*1 tbsp*	*1 tbsp*
Green apple, chopped	*1*	*1*	*1*
Lemon juice	*2 tbsp*	*2 tbsp*	*2 tbsp*

1. Mix all the ingredients together in a bowl and sprinkle with lemon juice.

Red Salad

	Metric	Imperial	American
Makes 2 portions			
Red cabbage, sliced	*¼ cabbage*	*¼ cabbage*	*¼ cabbage*
Carrots, grated	*2*	*2*	*2*
Red pepper, deseeded and chopped	*¼ pepper*	*¼ pepper*	*¼ pepper*
Raisins	*50 g*	*2 oz*	*⅓ cup*
Lemon juice	*2 tbsp*	*2 tbsp*	*2 tbsp*

1. Mix all the ingredients together in a bowl and sprinkle with lemon juice.

Cucumber and Apple Salad

Stir chopped cucumber and apple into natural yoghurt. If liked add walnuts or chopped hazelnuts.

Winter Salad

Grate carrots, apples and cucumber. Toss in some raisins and if liked some grated lemon rind (zest). Squeeze fresh lemon juice over the salad.

Carrot and Orange Salad

Slice carrots into short sticks. Cook lightly and drain. Wash an orange, grate the rind (zest) and sprinkle over the cooked carrots. Squeeze orange juice over the carrots. Sprinkle with chopped parsley.

Nutty Murphy

Boil some well scrubbed potatoes. Do not remove the skins. Dice when cold. Stir in some dry roasted peanuts and a sprinkling of sesame seeds.

Nuts n' Shoots

Mix chopped dates, diced apples, walnuts, bean sprouts and parsley.

Greek Cucumber Salad

Stir cubes of cucumber into natural yoghurt.

Ratatouille

Roughly chop equal quantities of onions, courgettes (zucchini), aubergines (eggplants) and sweet peppers. Simmer in a little olive oil for approximately 10 minutes. Add skinned chopped tomatoes (canned tomatoes will do) and a squeeze of garlic. Simmer for another 5 minutes. Sprinkle with fresh parsley and basil.

Potato, Radish and Nut Salad

Peel and boil a medium sized sweet potato. If using an ordinary potato, scrub but do not peel. Cool then dice. Stir in a few crisp and peppery pink radishes, adding a little more colour with some peas. Give this salad crunch by tossing in some chopped walnuts or hazelnuts. At the last minute pour over a yoghurt dressing.

Cauliflower Salad

Use raw or blanched cauliflower and break into very small florets. Mix with shredded lettuce or shredded Savoy cabbage. Sprinkle with sunflower seeds and parsley sprigs. A vinaigrette, the classic French dressing, goes well with this salad.

Vinaigrette

Make a vinaigrette with one part wine vinegar to three parts olive oil and black pepper to taste. Lemon juice may be used instead of the wine vinegar. Olive oil is expensive, but its subtle Mediterranean flavour adds a touch of dignity to the simplest dish. Look out for the "extra virgin olive oil", this is the oil from the first pressing recognisable by its green colour.

DRINKS

All supermarkets, corner shops and milkmen have plentiful supplies of pure unsweetened fruit juice, a must for all school lunch boxes.

Healthy eating should also mean healthy drinking, not so easy because most drink manufacturers as yet jealously guard the secrets of their additive rich drinks. Reading the side of the can is mostly uninformative. Chemicals are neatly disguised behind trade names.

Banana Shake

	Metric	Imperial	American
Makes 1 drink			
Banana, ripe	*1 large*	*1 large*	*1 large*
Vanilla essence (extract)	*few drops*	*few drops*	*few drops*
Honey			
Skimmed milk	*300 ml*	*½ pint*	*1¼ cups*

1. Place the banana, vanilla and honey to taste into a liquidizer or blender. Process until smooth.
2. With the liquidizer still running, gradually add the milk.
3. Chill until ready to transport.

Summer Fruit Drink

	Metric	Imperial	American
Makes 2 drinks			
Strawberries or other soft fruit	*100 g*	*4 oz*	*scant 1 cup*
Vanilla essence (extract)	*½ tsp*	*½ tsp*	*½ tsp*
Skimmed milk	*300 ml*	*½ pint*	*1¼ cups*
Water	*150 ml*	*¼ pint*	*⅔ cup*

1. Place the strawberries and vanilla essence into a liquidizer or blender. Process until smooth.
2. With the liquidizer still running gradually add the milk and water.
3. Chill until ready to transport.

Fruit Yoghurt Drink

	Metric	Imperial	American
Makes 1 drink			
Soft fruit of choice	*100 g*	*4 oz*	*1 cup*
Natural yoghurt	*300 ml*	*½ pint*	*1¼ cups*
Honey to taste			

1. Place the fruit, yoghurt and honey to taste into a liquidizer or blender. Process until smooth.
2. Chill until ready to transport.

Yoghurt Fruit Cup

	Metric	Imperial	American
Makes 2 drinks			
Banana	1	1	1
Wheatgerm	1 tsp	1 tsp	1 tsp
Egg	1	1	1
Natural yoghurt	300 ml	½ pint	1¼ cups
Orange juice	150 ml	¼ pint	⅔ cup
Water	150 ml	¼ pint	⅔ cup

1. Place the banana, wheatgerm, egg and yoghurt in a liquidizer or blender. Process until smooth.
2. With the liquidizer still running gradually pour on the orange juice and water.
3. Chill until ready to transport.

Fruit Surprise

	Metric	Imperial	American
Makes 2 drinks			
Juice of ½ lemon			
Orange juice	150 ml	¼ pint	⅔ cup
Grapefruit juice	150 ml	¼ pint	⅔ cup
Mineral water	300 ml	½ pint	1¼ cups

1. Mix all together in a jug. Chill until ready to transport.

Thirst Quencher

	Metric	Imperial	American
Makes 2 drinks			
Pineapple juice	*150 ml*	*¼ pint*	*⅔ cup*
Orange juice	*150 ml*	*¼ pint*	*⅔ cup*
Lemonade	*150 ml*	*¼ pint*	*⅔ cup*
Water	*150 ml*	*¼ pint*	*⅔ cup*

1. Mix all together in a jug. Chill until ready to transport.

Apple and Mint Refresher

	Metric	Imperial	American
Makes 2 drinks			
Water	*300 ml*	*½ pint*	*1¼ cups*
Apple juice	*1 tbsp*	*1 tbsp*	*1 tbsp*
Mineral water	*300 ml*	*½ pint*	*1¼ cups*
Fresh mint, chopped			

1. Mix the water and apple juice together.
2. Stir in the mint.
3. Chill until ready to transport.

Citrus Drink

1 part tropical fruit juice
1 part orange juice
1 part grapefruit juice
2 parts mineral water
lemon juice

1. Mix together the juices and water in a large jug. Add lemon juice to taste.
2. Chill until ready to transport.

Orange and Apple Drink

	Metric	Imperial	American
Makes 1 drink			
Apple juice	*300 ml*	*½ pint*	*1¼ cups*
Juice of orange	*1 large*	*1 large*	*1 large*
Lemon juice			

1. Mix the apple and orange juices together.
2. Add a few drops of lemon juice to taste.
3. Chill until ready to transport.

Lemon Barley Water

	Metric	Imperial	American
Makes 2 drinks			
Pearl barley	*50 g*	*2 oz*	*⅓ cup*
Water	*600 ml*	*1 pint*	*2½ cups*
Juice of lemons	*2*	*2*	*2*
Sugar or honey	*3 tbsp*	*3 tbsp*	*3 tbsp*

1. Place the barley in a saucepan filled with water and bring to the boil. Strain and rinse the barley.
2. Return barley to saucepan with the 600 ml/1 pint/2½ cups water. Bring to the boil and simmer for 1 hour.
3. Strain and stir in the lemon juice and sugar or honey.

Note: This keeps well stored in the refrigerator.

Hot Drinks

In winter hot drinks are a real comfort and make a welcome change from fruit juices and fizzy drinks. Made with skimmed milk they provide a valuable source of calcium. All the 'bedtime' drinks make delicious mid-day beverages.

BEST OF THE BARS AND ALTERNATIVE CRISPS

Watch out for bars that disguise sugar by using alternative names. Molasses, glucose, fructose, honey, treacle, cane syrup and invert sugar are all types of sugar.

Look for crisps which are additive free, low in fat and salt.

BARS

Castaway cereal bar – Holly Mill Bakery
Carob chip bar – Holly Mill Bakery
Apple and Cardamom bar – Holly Mill Bakery
Coconut bar – Shepherd Boy Ltd
Banana bar – Prewetts
Carob and Orange bar – Prewetts
Sesame Snaps – Blue Label
Crunchy bars – Jordans
Harvest Crunch – The Boots Company plc
Seed bar – The Boots Company plc
Natural Crunch – The Boots Company plc
Cluster cereal bar – Applefords

CRISPS

Nature's Choice (made from unpeeled potatoes)
Vico crisps

SPREADS AND DIPS

Sardine Spread

	Metric	Imperial	American
Can sardines in brine, drained	120 g	4¼ oz	4 oz
Natural yoghurt	2 tbsp	2 tbsp	2 tbsp
Low fat mayonnaise	2 tsp	2 tsp	2 tsp
Chopped parsley	1 tbsp	1 tbsp	1 tbsp
Few drops lemon juice			
Ground black pepper			

1. Blend all the ingredients together. Season with lemon juice and pepper to taste.

Cheese Spread

	Metric	Imperial	American
Cream cheese or quark (small curd cottage cheese)	100 g	4 oz	½ cup
Tomato	1	1	1
Low fat mayonnaise	1 tsp	1 tsp	1 tsp
Chopped mint	1 tsp	1 tsp	1 tsp

1. Blend all the ingredients together.

Vegetable Pâté and Mushrooms

	Metric	Imperial	American
Vegetable oil	1 tbsp	1 tbsp	1 tbsp
Mushrooms	50 g	2 oz	½ cup
Wholemeal (whole wheat) bread			
Tartex or vegetable pâté	1 tbsp	1 tbsp	1 tbsp
Tomato, sliced	1	1	1

1. Heat the oil in a saucepan and lightly sauté the mushrooms until just soft, about 4 minutes.
2. Spread slices of bread with Tartex. Arrange tomato on top and then finish with a layer of mushrooms.

Spiced Chicken Spread

	Metric	Imperial	American
Lean cooked chicken, chopped	100 g	4 oz	½ cup
Natural yoghurt	150 ml	5 fl oz	⅔ cup
Horseradish sauce	½ tsp	½ tsp	½ tsp
Carrot, grated	1 tbsp	1 tbsp	1 tbsp

1. Mix all the ingredients together.

FAST FILLINGS

No matter how well organised you intend to be there is always a time when the system breaks down. Without a doubt a hungry member of the family will grab the nearest bag from the freezer or gobble up the neatly packed salad intended for the next morning's lunch box. It is at these moments when old habits die hard and the first thing you reach for is the loaf of bread and sandwich spread. With this thought in mind, and because sandwiches can be exciting and nutritious with a few helpful suggestions, we have included a list of fillings for you to try.

COTTAGE CHEESE BASED

Cottage cheese with grated carrot and raisins
Cottage cheese with desiccated (shredded) coconut and honey
Cottage cheese with chopped celery and apple
Cottage cheese with chopped apricots
Cottage cheese with chopped dates and nuts

FISH BASED

Sardines mashed with hard-boiled (hard-cooked) egg and lemon juice
Sardines mashed with chopped cucumber and parsley
Tuna mashed with chopped cucumber and mayonnaise
Tuna mashed with chopped orange and mayonnaise
Tuna mashed with chopped tomato and mayonnaise

EGG BASED

Scrambled eggs with chopped mushrooms and tomatoes
Boiled egg, chopped with chives
Boiled egg, chopped with mayonnaise and curry powder

NUT BASED

Peanut butter and mashed banana
Peanut butter and chopped apple
Peanut butter and sweetcorn
Nut loaf and chopped tomato
Peanut butter and raisins
Peanut butter and slices of cooked chicken

CHEESE BASED

Low fat quark and chopped vegetables
Grated Cheddar, apple and raisins
Grated Cheddar, grated carrot and mayonnaise
Brie with chopped walnuts and lettuce

Index